Love
Out
Loud

Building a
Relationship and Family
from Scratch

Love
Out
Loud

Terrell & Jarius Joseph

LEGACY
LIT

Boston   New York

Copyright © 2024 by Terrell Joseph and Jarius Joseph

Cover design by Emily Mahon

Cover copyright © 2024 by Hachette Book Group, Inc.

Legacy Lit

Hachette Book Group

1290 Avenue of the Americas

New York, NY 10104

LegacyLitBooks.com

@LegacyLitBooks

First Edition: June 2024

Legacy Lit is an imprint of Grand Central Publishing. The Legacy Lit name and logo are registered trademarks of Hachette Book Group, Inc.

The publisher is not responsible for websites (or their content) that are not owned by the publisher.

The Hachette Speakers Bureau provides a wide range of authors for speaking events. To find out more, go to hachettespeakersbureau.com or email HachetteSpeakers@hbgusa.com.

Legacy Lit books may be purchased in bulk for business, educational, or promotional use. For information, please contact your local bookseller or the Hachette Book Group Special Markets Department at special.markets@hbgusa.com.

Library of Congress Cataloging-in-Publication Data has been applied for.

ISBNs: 978-1-5387-6688-0 (trade paperback); 978-1-5387-6689-7 (ebook)

Printed in the United States of America

LSC-C

Printing 1, 2024

To Our Children:
There is nothing in life we love nor want more
than you. You are everything we dreamt, prayed, and
sacrificed for. With the entirety of our hearts
and existence, we love you.

To Our Family:
Our love for you will always be infinite.
Thank you for the love you poured into us.

To Our T&J Fam:
We want you to know that without you,
none of this is possible. You have been the engine
that has kept us moving even when we did not
have the strength to keep going ourselves.
We love you deep!

Contents

Introduction

Our wedding was an evening that we will never forget. After months of planning, we somehow managed to pull off an intimate candlelight ceremony with our closest family and friends in a beautiful hotel in downtown Atlanta. If you've ever planned a wedding, you know how hard it can be to make your special day your own without going crazy. So it was truly a joy to walk into our venue and see the vision that we had only imagined finally come to life.

After we formally shared our vows and sealed our union, we had a huge surprise for our guests. For four months, we had been keeping the secret that we had become fathers to not one, but two beautiful children. After the devastating heartbreak of losing our first daughter, we kept the news of the births of our son and our second daughter incredibly private. But this night seemed like the perfect moment to share with our circle that not only were we making our union official, but we had become a family as well.

Neither one of us could stop the tears from flowing from our eyes as we walked into our reception holding Ashton and Aria in our arms. It was such a sweet release and celebration to finally be able to share the good news of their arrival with everyone we loved. It was such a beautiful moment of being surrounded by love in a way that we never could have imagined.

While the night of our wedding felt like a fairy tale come true, just five years earlier, we were college freshmen still becoming comfortable with our identities as gay men, figuring out this whirlwind love affair that we were stumbling and tumbling into every day, and just trying to find a place in the world. While we felt blessed to spark a once-in-a-lifetime romance that shocked even us at times, as two gay Black men from rural Louisiana, the last thing we were expecting was to find each other during our freshman year of college, and we continue to do the hard work every day to choose each other and create our own version of happily ever after.

Our love is far from practical, but we want the same things that most couples and families want. We all know what it's like to crave real love, the desire to feel welcome in a like-minded community, and the hope to walk through the world without judgment—all while wishing we could better listen to our inner voices and possess more self-awareness and authenticity. This type of existence is our human birthright, yet so many of us feel blocked from reaching the very desires that make us feel fulfilled. It can be a real challenge to form genuine relationships, create families, discover self-love, find support, pursue good intentions, find a spiritual community, take time to unwind, and feel comfortable in our own skin. In an ideal world, we'd chase these meaningful goals with creativity and an open heart, but far too often, social pressure and outdated opinions get in the way.

Choosing to write *Love Out Loud* together has taken an incredible amount of courage and vulnerability for us, but we believe that there is a lot that we can share and lessons that can be learned from our relationship. As a Black same-sex couple who have been together since we were eighteen years old—and more than a decade later, raising three thriving children—we are proof that whether you're out to find love, forge new paths, or find your people in a compatible community, there is always a way. In fact, through our popular social media platforms, we reach millions of individuals who love how we dispel so many everyday myths, especially about what love and same-sex families look like. Now this doesn't mean we haven't noticed a few cocked eyebrows at the grocery store or overheard stodgy microaggressions at the local coffee shop.

We've just learned how to understand and manage these moments with composure, compassion, perspective, and humor—and taught others how to do the same. We know how to inspire our audience to be better humans, and we have countless lessons to share about relationships, marriage, parenting, friendship, compassion, living your truth, communication, finding faith, dealing with shame, practicing forgiveness, and much more.

As thoughtful husbands, fathers, entrepreneurs, social media influencers, and philanthropists, we're proud to be examples of what it means to create a family outside of the modern American ideal. But we're also happy to let you in on our mistakes, challenges, and pitfalls, too. Our journey is not your everyday love story—and it hasn't always been a smooth road. Though our relationship began as friends in college, it quickly became romantic—and a big secret kept from friends and family. Jarius had already come out, but Terrell took some time before telling his mom that he was bisexual. Raised in the church, Jarius even broke up with Terrell for a spell, since his pastor said their partnership was an "abomination" to God; we clearly reunited but had to re-create our relationship with—and faith in—a God that was different than the one we were raised to know, and who accepted and loved us unconditionally.

When we moved to Atlanta after college, our relationship *remained* a secret even throughout our journey to become fathers. Our challenges and growth didn't stop there. When we got married, blending families was tough, since we were raised so differently. And seven years into our marriage, we had to deal with the fact that we were growing in opposite directions, and tough breaks with infidelity almost stopped our love story in its tracks. With a savvy counselor and plenty of self-help books, we had to let go of our expectations about what a traditional marriage would be to accommodate each other's views and needs. We found ourselves unlearning, and then relearning, what it meant to really love each other.

We've also wrestled with managing a complicated work–life balance, understanding what kind of parents we want to be and how to raise our kids in a healthy home, finding time to make memories, and ultimately building what we call our "chosen family." Through it all, our distinct choices have challenged us to be better people and truer to our souls. Against all odds, we've created the life we want.

We know that everyone enjoys a good love story, and we certainly have some juicy and adventurous tales from our journey that are sure to inspire and entertain you. But the biggest things we want you to walk away from this book with are the lessons that we learned from daring to be authentically ourselves. Throughout these pages, we will share with you some of the hard-won lessons that we gained about going through the challenges of learning each other's communication styles, discovering how to fight cleanly and fairly (and at times we're still recovering from fighting dirty and below the belt!), and understanding how to push each person in a relationship toward their dreams.

We will also let you into our challenges of what it meant to become proud gay fathers in a much different way than we ever imagined. Like many of you who are parents, we are sure that you came into parenthood with your own preconceptions of what it would be to raise a child. We want you to walk away with the power to give yourself grace and freedom to discover who your children are, uncover the kind of parent that you want to be, and not carry forward any generational patterns or challenges. Through our lessons, we want to empower you to have the freedom to make mistakes and to learn along with your children.

We also want you to walk away from this book

understanding and celebrating the power of finding your tribe—the people who will support your love and the family that you want to create. We're honestly still learning every day what that looks like for us in our family. But as we wade through the muddy waters of evolving our inner circle as we grow, hopefully you will be inspired to know that you can find your people for the different seasons and phases in your life, too.

While this book will dive into some of our deepest and darkest challenges, ultimately it is a celebration of what it means to find your person and to love them on your own terms. Particularly for people like us who are in the LGBTQIA+ community, we want you to have the tools, the inspiration, and the energy to love all of who you are and to do that in a way that you do not have to be ashamed of.

Loving out loud doesn't mean that you won't have days when you go to bed mad or bring your outside challenges through your front door. But loving out loud means that you're willing to do what it takes to fortify yourself and to get past the tough days. Loving out loud means that you're willing to take those hard knocks in your relationship and discover how to turn them into victories.

We want you to see yourselves in these stories and know that if we can make it through some of our toughest times, you can, too. Each and every chapter will not only include our life story and experiences, but also reveal lessons that you can use in your own life and that will hopefully enable you to keep growing and be strengthened within your own relationship.

This book certainly isn't a definitive guide or a blueprint of how to do things our way. We're still falling down and scraping our knees as we go along the way, too. So we certainly don't think that we're experts. But through every challenge, we've become stronger, more resilient, and more determined to laugh out loud, to live in our truth, and inspire others along the way.

We wrote *Love Out Loud* so that families like ours could have hope. We wrote this book so that you could understand that if you are creating your life, your love, and your business outside of the box, we're here to show you that it's not impossible. If two young boys from rural Louisiana could make their wildest dreams come true, there's no reason why you can't do it, too.

Love
Out
Loud

1

Breaking All
the Rules

Growing up in the Deep South, we didn't have the language or the experiences to understand who we were as young, gay, Black boys. Even in the early 2000s, there weren't comfortable spaces in our hometowns to build community with other LGBTQIA+ kids or to date without the fear of judgment. What we did have early in adolescence were dreams that went far beyond the limitations of what our hometowns could provide. This is not to say that we did not love the unique and rich traditions that came from being raised in Louisiana. However, what our Southern upbringing had an abundance of in culture, it lacked in perspectives, resources, and the safety we needed to live our truth at the time.

There was something for both of us that was yearning to live life beyond the shadows of secrecy and to discover how to live our lives out loud. And to nurture that special something, we needed to be exposed to new perspectives and environments that supported the parts of us that were nonnegotiables—we needed to get out, like yesterday.

Our small-town upbringings could have easily left us stuck in limited conversations and possibilities for our future. But both of us sowed seeds of tenacity that needed to grow. So we took what we loved from Louisiana, and we leaped into a bigger life.

In this chapter, we will begin peeling back the layers of both of our childhoods, the difficulties of being fully expressed at home and in our communities, and the decisions that led us to leave home and take on the adventure of growing from boys to men.

Jarius

The choice to leave my hometown was very simple for me. I grew up in a town where most of the people around me had little to no ambition. After high school graduation, most of my classmates started working the only jobs that were available, which were CNAs and cooks at the casino. It was the same story over and over again, and I honestly wanted no part of it. And when it came to the dating scene, it was full of recycled high school flings—pairs who sometimes couldn't even stand each other but who got together anyway because there were literally no other options. I knew that if I didn't get out, I could see my life following that same pattern.

Even at a young age, I believed that there was no way I was going to prosper any further within the confines of the 4,000 people in my hometown. I *had* to go out and find my way, even if that meant being uncomfortable in a brand-new place where I did not know anyone. And there wasn't any way in hell that I was going to risk not making my dreams become a reality. Truthfully, I didn't even know exactly what I wanted to do when I grew up, but knew I wanted to do amazing things, and I knew that if I didn't move away, I was never going to figure out my sexuality and discover what was going on with me internally.

Now, before we get too deep in the story, I'd like to mention that there is absolutely nothing wrong with staying in your hometown. Hell, somebody has to live there, right? I just knew it wasn't for me, and that is also okay. Now that the disclaimer has been made and I don't have to worry about getting jumped when I go back home, let's continue with the story.

In my quest to find myself, I grew interested in exploring guys romantically, but I couldn't explore that curiosity safely or without fear and judgment. I remember as early as elementary school that any boy who showed any traits that were remotely "feminine" was immediately bullied. So, while everyone around me was paging through the yearbook for their potential spouse, homophobia in my hometown required me to move in secrecy and suppress whatever feelings I might have been experiencing for guys.

My path to understanding my sexuality was especially complicated, particularly when it came to my mom. My mother tussled with her sexuality throughout most of my childhood. She dated women privately for the same reasons: fear of judgment. My family didn't really talk about things that disrupted their worldview, so it became so hush-hush that I felt like I had to hide. The more I saw my mom dating or hanging out with women, the more I felt like I was holding on to this huge secret for her. When my mom was out on a date, I always felt like I had to come up with a lie about where she was when my grandmother called to check on me. There were other times when my mother would bring me with her when she was dating someone in another town or when she was visiting someone on the weekend. This was short-lived because I never liked any of the women she dated. There were more than a few times when she got into physical altercations with the women she was dating and I found myself caught in the middle. Even though I always felt like she could have chosen a better partner to be with, I surely wasn't about to let nobody take down my mama!

In the ninth grade, I officially started feeling more of an attraction to men. I clearly knew that there was something rising in me when I was around other boys, but I also knew that expressing my true interests out loud at that point could lead to being bullied or singled out. So when I was bold enough to express my interest in someone, I knew that I had to keep it private. One of the guys I started to take an interest in left me a voice mail on my cell phone. And because I always stayed in trouble for little things with my mom, she knew that the worst punishment for me at the time was taking away my phone.

While I was being punished, she went into my phone and heard a voice mail from a guy who said that he loved me. When she straight up asked me if I was talking to this guy, I came back with a hot teenage attitude and told her, "Yes, I am." We got into a huge argument. I was actually quite surprised that she wasn't more supportive and understanding that this was my way to my truth. And here I'd been carrying her secret for years. How could she not have the heart to understand what I was going through? When we finally settled down after that argument, I remember my mother asking me, "Why would this be anyone else's business but your own? Nobody else doesn't need to know about that part of you." I started to think, *If my mother is living her life in secrecy, what does that mean for me?*

Looking back, I now understand my mother was living in fear. She couldn't support me the way I needed because she didn't have the tools to support that part of herself. And that honestly makes me empathize with her even more.

Terrell

For as long as I can remember, I have been a rule breaker. Now don't get me wrong, I was a great kid, but I've always liked being able to make my own choices. I've never wanted to feel like someone or something has control over me in any way. For example, when it was time for me to head out to college, I did all the research myself for filling out my financial aid forms and applying to the colleges that felt like the right fit for me. I didn't want my parents' input at all when it was time for me to make that decision. I always felt different, from the way I thought, the way I managed my money, and even to my big goals and aspirations.

I grew up in a very traditional household that was based on middle-class, Southern, Christian morals and standards. Both of my parents were focused on me and my sister getting "good jobs" that we could eventually retire from one day, similar to what they were trying to accomplish for themselves. That was not on my bingo card! I dreamed of owning my own business, having the office with a view in a skyscraper that I would ride to each day in the back of my stretch limousine. Needless to say, I recognized early on that as long as I lived there, I eventually was going to need to find a way to do my own thing.

It also did not help that my parents did not have a very healthy relationship when I was growing up. Their marriage and how they coexisted was not anything that I aspired to replicate. I truly believed that they loved each other but had grown apart. And the only reason they were still together was to provide a sense of normalcy for my sister and me.

My dad and I also butted heads a lot. Most of our arguments came from the independent spirit I told you about previously. As most of us have heard at least once in our lives, I was reminded by my dad that "This is my house, and as long as you are under my roof, these are my rules." Every day I was thinking, *Well, I need to figure out a way* not *to be under your roof!* For a lot of my childhood, I started checking out mentally to protect my sanity, and I was always in search of how to find and create my own independence.

Although it would take me a while to discover exactly what I wanted to do, I just knew that my hometown wasn't going to give me the environment and the opportunities that I needed to live out these big dreams that were bubbling inside me. And while I would never tear down anyone who decided to stay in my hometown, I just knew that there was more for me, and if I wanted to keep my sanity, I owed it to myself to break outside of those boundaries and discover what the world had to offer me.

As I was discovering more about who I was in high school, I learned I was attracted to guys. Although I didn't act on it until later in high school, the feelings were definitely there. It didn't help that I wasn't as overly macho as the other guys around me, either. I would hear the whispers of people saying, "I wonder if he is gay." In my teenage years, I certainly wasn't ready to answer that question.

During my senior year of high school, I started secretly talking with this guy who I liked—or at least I *thought* I liked. But just a few weeks into dating, he expressed that he wanted us to be official. I realized that he'd caught serious feelings that I didn't share. I mean, he was fine, but I just couldn't see a future dating a guy in my hometown. At that time, I didn't want to take the risk of being outed or someone whispering about us being together. I didn't quite know what to do with my feelings with men at the time. So I immediately shut down our nonrelationship. In that moment, I felt like my actions were super selfish, but I also knew that I needed to be in an environment where I could get away from all those speculations and assumptions about who I was and who I wanted to be—I needed an environment where I could thrive.

When it was time for me to choose where I wanted to go to college, Louisiana State University (LSU) felt like the perfect choice to make a fresh start. We had a running joke in my high school that our local college was like "Going to High School, Part Two." I didn't want to have the same experience around the same people. To avoid out-of-state fees and maximize my scholarships, I knew I'd have to pick a school in Louisiana, but I still needed to create some distance.

I was so excited to be going to a school where nobody would know me, and I could start over. Going to LSU would be my opportunity to be whoever I wanted to be and do whatever I wanted to do.

Lesson No. 1: It's Okay to Assess the World Around You

We both discovered that in order for us to keep growing and evolving, we had to leave our hometowns. For those of you who may be feeling boxed in by your current city, your job, your house of worship, or anywhere else that you've outgrown, it's more than okay to assess the world around you and decide to make different choices. You have the right to make choices that are in service of your joy and your happiness—and you don't have to make any apologies for that.

Jarius

When I was fifteen, I visited a friend's home in a trailer park. When I got to my friend's trailer, I knocked on their door but no one answered. After knocking for a while, I noticed that there was a man sitting outside the very next trailer. When I asked him, he said that he didn't know where my friend and their family were or when they'd be back, but then he asked me, "So where all the girls be at down here?" I replied, "I have no idea." Then he said, "Well, what about the guys?" My heart dropped. Did this man really just ask me that? I felt so many things at that moment, but I chose to pretend like I didn't hear him. So I said, "What?" He replied, "Never mind, bro."

Initially I walked away, but then my intrigue started creeping in and I walked back to him to see where all of this could go. This was so embarrassing for me, because I had walked all the way back to the street, and there I was walking all the way back to talk to a man I didn't even know existed ten minutes ago.

We talked a little bit more and I agreed to follow him into a deserted area behind the trailer park. Looking back now, I think that man had to be every bit of twenty-one or twenty-two years old, and I should not have been talking to him in the first place. But my curiosity got the best of me and we had oral sex in this field without another soul around us for miles. Although he was very nice and I was attracted to him physically, I felt so disgusted when we were done. I was angry at myself for even getting into this dangerous situation where I could have contracted an STI or, worse, been killed. I wanted to be able to love out loud, have someone who loved me for me, and not have to keep them in the shadows.

––––––––––

Leaving home gave us the independence that we needed at the time. Even though we were still in Southern college towns that were not super progressive, leaving our small hometowns allowed us to see ourselves from a much larger viewpoint and it gave us more freedom. So we both learned that oftentimes you have to go and separate yourself from the group in order to reach your full potential.

We also went to college with radically different experiences around coming out and being comfortable with dating men. Jarius came out to his mother at fifteen, and Terrell was a junior in college before he sent a text message—of all things!—to his mother to share his truth. We were definitely coming out from opposite ends of the spectrum.

And while you would think that it would have been easier for Jarius coming out to a mother who dated women, his experiences were just as difficult, if not more so, than Terrell's. Jarius had to come to the realization that because his mother was still having internal conflicts about her own sexuality, he couldn't expect her to be okay with that part of herself being brought out in her child. He was definitely still working through the trauma of holding in her secret while trying to find his own truth.

Terrell had a much different experience. He was able to sit down and talk with his mother. After he sent the text message to her, his mother was very supportive, and he was able to share more about his sexuality. But one of the first things that she asked in their conversations was, "Well, son, did someone molest you?" That question initially made him very uncomfortable because far too many parents make that assumption. He had to break it down and be clear with her that his sexuality wasn't due to abuse and that she didn't have to feel responsible or that she could have done anything differently.

We also had to move past our resentment of seeing our gay white peers, who were able to be out and more open while we still had to hide in the shadows of calling each other "roommates." Terrell attended LSU, which was a predominantly white campus, while Jarius attended Southern University, which was a historically Black college. At first, we would always feel envious because we didn't know the backstories of those gay white students and why they were able to live in their truth while we weren't. It made us question, "Would we be farther along in our truth if we came from different families or different backgrounds?"

Now, it would take us another five years to go beyond telling folks that we were just roommates, but our simple willingness to leave home made it possible for both of us to do whatever we wanted to do. While we didn't go to college necessarily to find love, eventually meeting each other in college allowed us to be open enough to explore a relationship between the two of us, without having to reveal our relationship to the masses until we were ready. We sure 'nough wouldn't have been able to do that in either one of our hometowns.

Lesson No. 2: If All You See Is All You Know, How Will You Grow?

When you're a person who thinks much larger than the people around you, you'll always feel like a black sheep. We know that it takes an incredible amount of courage to separate yourself from the group in order to reach your full potential. It is more than okay to break a cycle of small and limited thinking. But we have both been firm believers in knowing that if all you see is all you know, you'll never know how much you can grow. Your changes and choices don't have to be as large as ours. We are not, and we repeat NOT, telling anyone to quit their job or to leave their marriage tomorrow. But we are giving you a permission slip to start looking at your life and truly seeing if where you are now is helping you to explore your greatest dreams and be the best you can be.

And if you feel called to start making changes, start small. Your baby steps can be reaching out to someone in a field that you want to work in or making one social media post this week about a new business that you want to venture into. Nothing is impossible. But those changes will happen only if you're courageous enough to know that you deserve to have the life that you want.

2

You Can't Build on a
Broken Foundation

Who would have thought that we would spark a lifelong romance at a haunted house during Halloween? We'd met a few weeks earlier on a cold, crisp night at the beginning of October. We were both still getting settled into our first semester as freshmen and beginning to explore dating and making connections with people outside of our hometowns for the first time. The night we met, there was a little bit more than just flirtation spinning in the air. However, when we were invited to a haunted house by our mutual friends and a few of our respective cousins a few weeks later, we all arrived with our respective girl-friends and boyfriends at the time.

Our group had such a great time at the haunted house that we decided to keep the party going and grab some food at a local restaurant. After everyone was seated at our table, somehow our chairs were close together and those sparks that we'd felt in the haunted house continued to grow. While we were being cool, friendly, and open with the whole group, whenever we had a few moments to talk directly with each other, we could tell that we had a lot in common and that the energy between us flowed easily.

While the larger group was having conversations about upcoming football games and other parties on campus, we naturally ventured off into our own discussions about fashion, what it felt like to be freshmen, leaving our hometowns for the first time, and having the freedom to begin seeing our lives in completely different ways. Jarius always jokingly says that it was Terrell's flirting with him about his letterman jacket at the time that sparked the beginning of our connection. We also talked about how we were seeing the freedom white gay students at our respective schools had to be out and open while many of our Black gay peers were still living in the shadows.

While the vibes were certainly right for romance when we met, after that night at the haunted house, we did not keep in touch. In fact, when Jarius crossed paths with Terrell at the mall a few weeks later Terrell did not recognize Jarius at all! We exchanged Twitter accounts that night, and a friendship started to blossom when we soon realized that we just happened to live one street over from one another. What a coincidence, given that Jarius's school was across town. What are the odds he would be the next street over? Sounds like GOD's plan to us!

Close to almost two months later, our friendship accelerated into a full-on relationship.

With us totally boo'd up, each for the first time with a man, we knew, almost instinctively, that we had very real challenges to face together. How do you keep the sparks going when they're shrouded in secrecy, self-doubt, and fear? What does it take to bring two people together when you come from completely different environments? And does love truly conquer all in the end? In this chapter, we're going to dig into the lessons we had to learn about discovering who we were becoming as young men, the joy of sparking new love, and how we had to learn to build our love through the challenges of a broken foundation.

Jarius

Once I got to college, I felt liberated. I was finally in a place where, if I wanted to explore with a guy, whether that meant flirting, having a good friendship, or making a sexual connection, I could do so without the pressure of worrying if it would sweep like breaking news across the city. I could honestly ask myself, "Does this personality trait work for me?" or "Or do I like it when this guy tries this specific thing out with me?" I felt free to make my own decisions without having to look over my shoulder or be worried that I was going to become the topic of conversation.

Before meeting Terrell, I was dating someone on and off during and after my senior year of high school. He lived in the same town where I was attending college, so it seemed perfect. I was so excited to start exploring dating him with more freedom, but let me tell y'all, that relationship was toxic AF! I had so much anger built up during that relationship because he was emotionally immature. We had grown up in totally different environments and that contributed to a breakdown in emotional expression. On the one hand, I was the type who usually fought a lot: I wasn't afraid to be confrontational and said my piece whenever I could. On the other hand, he grew up in a chaotic home where he didn't have a voice and was surrounded by drama, so he didn't tolerate it in his adult life. We couldn't have been more opposite, but somehow it worked, or at least I thought it did. I suppressed so much of my anger, frustration, and combativeness because I liked him—until one day it all came out. He was supposed to come to my high school graduation but went missing for two whole days. I felt angry, hurt, and betrayed. This was going to be my official coming out and he went completely ghost. When we finally did speak, I was enraged and let it all out on him. I told him it was over and hung up the phone.

And just as I was settling into college life and I knew that I was ready to move on from that situation, I met Terrell. He immediately felt like such a sweet, genuine, and understanding person, and he was the total opposite of this toxic relationship that I was in. Being around Terrell just made more sense to me. I loved that his personality was more compatible with mine. I also liked that he was down for what I called my "hood escapades," when I wanted to have a little adventure. That made me feel more comfortable with him. From the moment we met, there was this spark, and I knew that something more was there for us.

Terrell

Y'all know that fresh start that I thought attending LSU was going to be? Well, that didn't last for long! Coming from my parents' house and their rules, I was ready to do whatever I wanted in college—party, date, and party again! Of course, my ultimate goal was to graduate, but I could do that and have fun, right? My new, fun life lasted all of two weeks before I met Jarius. I always jokingly say that he snatched away my freedom and tried to tie me down before all the campus cuties got their shot. However, after more than a decade together, our relationship and family have given me more freedom and happiness than all the club hopping and nights that I am sure I would have regretted could provide. Still, like any sensible—and admittedly guarded—late teen, I had more than a few doubts in the beginning.

But I was holding true to my "fresh start." I would pretend like I didn't understand his questions about my sexuality and acted oblivious to his forwardness. He was pressing me hard and I was dodging those advances like a pro athlete. Truthfully, I was nervous as hell but I liked everything about him. While I was open to exploring and satisfying my curiosity with him, I didn't know if being out and open with a man was what I was looking for. I would reel my feelings in and pull back every time I felt myself becoming vulnerable.

Even though Jarius and I were both in relationships when we met (I was low-key still dating a girl from my hometown), the vibes and the connection were there for both of us from the beginning. At the time, I still wasn't out, and while I know this sounds crazy, I wanted to have a girlfriend so I could still have the option to fit in while I was discovering exactly what I wanted to do with my burgeoning attraction toward men.

And all these feelings became increasingly persistent because Jarius was pursuing me hard! He let me know right from the beginning that he was feeling me, which was unlike anything I was used to. Still, I was holding true to my "fresh start." I told him more than once that I couldn't see anything happening for me with him.

But Jarius was fun! I loved that we both had similar experiences being from a small town and that we could spend hours together talking about everything and nothing. We were still discovering who we were and what we wanted to do with our lives, so I know that our conversations weren't especially heavy or deep, but Jarius made me happy. I was a pizza delivery driver during my freshman year, and I remember calling him during all my deliveries just to talk, even if it was for five minutes.

I knew I wanted him to be a part of my life, but not in that way. I had never been with a man out in the open, and I didn't want to be pushed into anything during my first semester in college, where I was supposed to be enjoying my freedom. It wasn't until Jarius outright asked me, "What are we doing, Terrell?" that I knew I had to be truthful—with myself and with him. I had not expected Jarius and me to grow so close so quickly, but it was undeniable that this was something special, and I had to allow myself to be more open with how I was feeling about him. I knew that if I kept playing this game of acting like I really didn't like him (when I knew deep down I did!), I would lose him. The clock was ticking, and I needed to make a decision.

Building Your Love After the Honeymoon

Terrell

Well, now here we are in a full-on relationship as two closeted gay Black men in college. While I really liked him, I was super reluctant to find out how this would go. Every emotional and sexual experience we'd had with a same-sex partner had been a secret that we'd worked hard to keep. Even something as seemingly small as holding hands turned into a huge deal for us. Jarius simply wanted to hold my hand one day while we were walking in the mall, but I refused. He hurtfully replied, "But if I was a girl, you wouldn't have any problem holding her hand. So why are we any different?" It was like Jarius wanted to turn a blind eye to consequences because he strongly believed that we deserved the same things as straight couples. But ultimately we both knew that it wasn't the smartest thing for us to be openly affectionate in Louisiana as gay Black men.

As I mentioned previously, we lived separately and one street over from each other. But then the cousin who was initially my roommate decided to move back home, and that created an opportunity for Jarius to move in. We could really be adults, enjoy our dating bliss, and now live together! To give ourselves a sense of "space" while keeping up the illusion that we were just roommates, we had separate rooms. However, we would often take turns sleeping in the other's room. Nothing could go wrong, right? *Wrong!*

One of the funniest moments during the beginning of our relationship was the night that we decided to have sex for the first time. I was always super cautious and borderline paranoid about making sure no one saw us when we were together. I always made sure we closed all the laptops around us and that the windows and doors were shut for fear that we'd be outed. Pretty strange, right? That night, Jarius was doing his college best to wine and dine me. He knew that whenever we made it there, it would be my first time having sex with a man. We had dinner at his apartment, where he was so nervous he totally messed up the entire meal. I pretended it was amazing, though, because he really did try. Shortly after dinner, we moved to the living room and started making out on the couch.

We got a little more comfortable and took things to the bedroom. But as soon as we both were undressed and ready to go all the way, we heard loud banging on the door. We both froze and had no idea what was going on. Now, you have to know I was literally losing it. I just told you guys how I was closing all the doors and windows and now someone was at the door while I was naked? My soul left my body for a moment.

The banging continued and then we heard a loud voice yelling, "Jarius, I know you're in there. I see your car. Come out now!" It was Jarius's ex-boyfriend pounding on the door! Here we were worried about cell phone and laptop cameras and now we are in the middle of the most hood sh— ever. Mood: ruined. Apparently he had been blowing up Jarius's cell phone while we were eating dinner, so we had no clue that he'd be coming over in a rage. Now, the raunchy side of me contemplated opening that door and immediately swinging, but, again, I was butt naked, and I was trying to keep my cool because Jarius looked like he had seen a ghost.

Jarius

Lemme tell you, the first thing that came to my mind when I saw Terrell's horrified face was, "This man is about to leave and never about to f— with me again— literally!" My first time with someone I really, truly had feelings for could've been ruined by my ex.

There was no way that he could have known I was in there with Terrell, and I can see now that he had probably come over to my apartment in a rage because I had ended things so abruptly with him.

Terrell and I stayed super quiet—and still naked— while my ex continued to pound on the door. Fortunately, after a little while, he left. I turned around and instantly melted into Terrell, embarrassed. I felt awful for putting him in that situation.

Nothing like that had ever happened to me in my life. But Terrell was very understanding and super sweet about it. He had the option to leave and follow my ex right down the driveway. I knew that he really liked me because when I explained how I messed up in thinking I could get out of my other relationship quickly and drama free, all he did was hold me and say, "Come here. It doesn't matter."

Lesson No. 3: Breaking Old Patterns

We had to learn that it was more than okay to break old patterns and learn how to see things differently together. Especially with us being so secretive in the first part of our relationship, we didn't know how to come out of those old patterns that we had brought with us to college.

As you are going into new environments throughout your life, there will be moments when you have to challenge yourself to go beyond what you know and to be brave enough to do something that you've never done before.

Codependent AF

We started to struggle with understanding how we were going to manage our relationship and what we wanted. Jarius was ready to risk it all while Terrell still was adamant about being in the closet.

The first few weeks of officially dating were bliss—with tons of boo-loving. It would be nothing for us to spend days together while skipping classes and discovering new ways to impress each other. But we also started to grow very quickly, and the honeymoon phase of our relationship was rapidly fading. Before we knew it, our mindsets shifted on what our relationship should look like long term.

During this time, we each started to really dive deep into learning more about the other person. We were discovering our "icks" as well as things we really loved about each other. For example, Jarius has always been particular about keeping shoes out of the living area while Terrell has always been a stickler about cleaning the kitchen after we finish cooking together. Given that we were strangers who fell for each other in this whirlwind of a situation, we really put our best foot forward in the beginning. But it's only so long that you can keep up the go-with-the-flow act in the name of love.

Terrell

I started to feel like our home was the only place we could be ourselves and where we didn't have to pretend to be roommates. I believe this started our codependency. We unintentionally started to see our friends less and less because we were so infatuated with each other. So we became each other's go-to person. We felt like all we needed was each other and we were content with that. This became a recipe for disaster once the honeymoon stage was over and we had to really do the work to make sure we didn't fail in college and have to move back home with our parents. This created its own issues because this was my first same-sex relationship, and I felt everyone was interested in my man! I didn't trust anyone!

Looking back on it, I know that this was very childish and immature, but I did not like the thought of a lot of male friends because my "gaydar" was still developing and I couldn't tell who had good intentions and who was trying to get down with the get down. So the easiest thing to do was to get rid of anyone who could potentially pose a threat to our relationship. Which in this case meant any other guys.

While we never had "gender roles," I felt as though I tried hard to be a great boyfriend. I also felt that I needed to overcompensate because of keeping us a secret. However, Jarius had baggage from a previous relationship that reared its ugly head in ours. I was very passive in my relationship but a firecracker everywhere else. Jarius was with someone previously who did not like conflict at all. Therefore, he kept a lot of his emotions bottled up in that relationship in order to keep it, and by the time we got together, the first sign of conflict with us became a *war*! While arguments were not fun, we always found our way through them. I had gone against everything I had been raised to believe as it relates to relationships with the opposite sex and against the commitment I'd made to myself because of my feelings for him. That was special; there was something there that I wasn't ready to let go of because this was huge for me.

So our little nineteen-year-old selves did our best to figure it out and communicate as best we knew how. This was before therapy was a topic that is as widely spoken about as is it today, but also who was going to listen to two little gay Black boys talk through their relationship drama? We were in this by ourselves, and if we wanted it to work, we had to put our egos aside and talk. Living under the same roof forced us to talk through our issues at an accelerated rate for our age. During these times, while stressful, we learned a lot about each other and how to better navigate each other's nonnegotiables.

After a few months of living together, we started getting into arguments every week. With all of our stress from school, coupled with the responsibilities of life, and navigating a new relationship, we ended up butting heads quite a bit. Soon, we were in the middle of a terrible rough patch.

I started to notice that he would text me that he was staying at work late, but I felt like something wasn't adding up. It drove me so far up the wall that I had to revert to my old detective ways. I always felt that my calling in life was to be an attorney or a detective. And I was on the hunt like an episode of *Blue's Clues,* looking for anything to calm my suspicions.

One night, I cooked dinner for us and cleaned up the apartment to set the mood while he was at work. I wanted us to talk and get to a better place and see if we could turn the tide. But when he got home, I just knew something wasn't right. I outright asked him if he was talking with someone else because I felt it in my spirit, and he was truthful and told me that he was interested in one of his coworkers. My heart shattered into a million pieces. I did not know how to respond to that. What was I going to say in that moment? I politely stood up and calmly walked to my room. Thinking back, it was really strange how calm I was. I cried for a bit and then my sadness turned into pure rage. Who? How? Why? A million questions popped into my head and they wouldn't go away. I needed answers. So I did what any of y'all would do...I took his phone while he was asleep and went through it. I know, I know. A total breach of privacy. But there it was—he was flirting with someone at his job. And to make things worse, the dude was in one of my classes at school. Y'all, I couldn't believe it but there it was. Immediately, I woke him up to confront him and that's when all hell broke loose. It very much gave Angela Bassett in *Waiting to Exhale*, and I completely lost it.

This was my first same-sex relationship. I couldn't believe this was happening and decisions needed to be made. I called his mother and said, "If you truly love your son, you will get here NOW, because I am about to do something I will likely regret." I was, quite literally, losing it.

After that, we contemplated moving out of our apartment and figuring things out separately. Even passing him in the hallway triggered me and I wanted to fight. Honestly, it was a really low point for us. We would have small conversations as we tried to figure out if this could work. But it all seemed to go south. How do you get over the one person who you felt safe enough to come out to—and who also deceived you in the worst possible way?

We finally got to a point where we put our anger aside and we were able to talk. Internally I had to be real and ask myself, "Do I really want to start over? Do I want to put myself back out there with another man? Would someone else be comfortable with me not being full 'out' yet?" I struggled a lot with those questions.

I really did love Jarius, but I still didn't know if we could truly make things work. From that point on, I created a lot of stipulations for our relationship. Jarius did not get the same Terrell twice, and it changed the trajectory of our relationship moving forward. If I was going to stay in this relationship, I needed to feel reassurance.

Jarius

Starting off our relationship with so much secrecy around us barred us from a real opportunity to set up a proper foundation based on what we really wanted. While it was cute in the beginning to be coy and unsure about committing to the relationship, the act got old real quick. Without a solid commitment, I feared that all Terrell wanted to do was play around with me. And when he was done, he would go on about his business, chasing his dreams like the rebel he is while I pined for his love. I knew that I wanted and deserved more than that.

When Terrell asked me flat out if I was cheating on him my heart sank, but I tried to overcompensate for the fear by having a badass attitude. I felt like I was back in the same situation as I was when I came out to my mom, and I just blurted out the truth. I had no choice but to be honest and stand in it. In that moment, giving him the response the way I gave it, I was trying to protect myself, but I didn't realize that it was going to break him. While things weren't great, he was truly someone I cared for. To see him break in front of me truly broke my heart.

Not only had I been caught, but I felt completely terrible about it. Here I was keeping *two* people a secret from each other. I knew that was creating a recipe for disaster. That really changed everything for us going forward. I wanted to redeem myself because I felt bad about what I had done to him, but I also wanted to redeem *myself* for falling into the same trap that had been modeled for me by the men in my family since I was a child. Terrell was a great guy—handsome, ambitious, and super smart—and I was willing to do whatever needed to be done to earn back his trust and better myself in the process. I was naïve to think this was going to be easy, not fully knowing the pain I caused him.

I loved him and I wanted to make him feel safe and secure. Little did I know that codependency has a funny way of coming to the surface. While my intentions sounded good, I truly believe a lot of our codependency started in the aftermath of my cheating. I was now committed to being an open book with Terrell, and I started spending the least amount of time on school as possible so that I could hurry up and get home to him. We had now created this new way of existing in our relationship that turned out to not be healthy for either one of us. But despite my best efforts, I felt like I was never going to overcome that mountain.

Like most people when you first fall in love, the first few weeks and months of our relationship felt like we were sliding down rainbows and galloping on unicorns. We wanted to spend every waking moment with each other. Now, more than a decade into our relationship, we can admit that, during the first few years, we were codependent and we didn't know how to be independent of each other without making our relationship more complicated.

When we started our relationship, we were super flirty with each other, we were having lots of sex, and all we wanted to do was stay in bed with each other all day. But when we realized that we were both failing several classes and that Terrell had to attend summer school, we knew that we couldn't be laid up under one another all day long anymore.

We both knew that we didn't want to go back

home, so we did what we needed to do to turn our grades around. All the while, we were still struggling with how to build our love on this broken foundation. Following our first infidelity, Jarius worked overtime to make Terrell feel safe and secure, while Terrell completely shifted and almost seemed turned off from the relationship. And just like any anxious and avoidant couple, we had to figure out how those characteristics were impacting our relationship.

Maybe to somebody else, that kind of behavior at the beginning of a relationship, especially when either one of us could have called it quits, might sound toxic. The beautiful side of that hard, messy work was that, time and time again, we constantly chose each other and were committed to finding a way to connect and reconnect. In a weird way, our traumas forced us to stay together and work them out.

It was time for us to learn how to show up and speak up and really communicate what we wanted out of our relationship.

Lesson No. 4: You Can't Build on a Broken Foundation

Sometimes someone will change their Facebook status and rant and rave about how their ex "wasted six months of my life." But did you really take the time during the dating stage to see if their energy was going to be something that you could deal with day in and day out? If they needed constant texting communication from you, were you honest with yourself about whether you were able to meet that need? If not, you can't blame the other person for wasting your time if you were not honest about what is important to you.

We also certainly didn't get to create a love story for more than twelve years without being willing to ask the hard questions—and being willing to deal with the small stuff, too. One of Jarius's pet peeves was Terrell leaving his shoes at the door. Jarius didn't see the point of having a pile of junk loading up at the front door when you could simply take them to the closet. While this sounds like an incredibly small and piddly thing to be annoyed about, you would be surprised by how minor preferences like this can explode when you don't take the time to really talk about things that are important to you. Eventually, in the spirit of compromise and meeting each other halfway, we worked to knock out the little things in hopes that the big things wouldn't be as hard.

We've also had to give each other the space to grow and change. We met each other at age eighteen, and now moving into our thirties, we are much different people than who we were as college freshmen. If you are not willing to acknowledge and recognize that your partner is going to change over time, it's quite possible that being in a long-term relationship could be challenging for you.

We've had to learn over time how to move as a unit. Not that we haven't had periods in our relationship where Terrell is speeding ahead into a new idea or project and Jarius is thoughtfully thinking about the next step, but we had to learn that there will be different versions of us and different seasons of our lives.

We eventually knew what we wanted—a loving marriage, kids, a good living, a stable life for our children, a happy home, and our version of the American Dream. When Terrell finally felt ready to jump into marriage and kids, Jarius's more traditional values wanted to ensure that we were first financially secure, had a nice house, and had other safe priorities in place before sharing a last name and starting our baby-making adventure.

It was also essential to establish a safe space for us to continue growing our love for each other and feel comfortable in our own skin. It's funny to think back on how Terrell's father drove a U-Haul with our stuff in it from Louisiana to our Georgia home, all while believing we were platonic roommates. Terrell still wasn't ready to come out to everyone in his family, especially since they'd always known him to have girlfriends and held certain expectations about what his future might look like. So we finally decided that while our college friends partied, dated, and figured out their careers, we'd start by buying a beautiful home together in Georgia, right after graduation. Stereotypes against the gay community can cause young gay men to think they'll never have a family or a monogamous, long-term partner. In our minds, we wanted to create our own family unit to defy the odds.

If you've been in a relationship or married for a minute, we're probably preaching to the choir a little bit over here. But it never hurts to be reminded that there will be times when you have growing pains in your relationship. You have to decide whether you're going to weather those changes, and if you have the patience to be able to thoughtfully move your partner along in the process as you are evolving as a couple.

While the speed of our relationship felt a little bit like a Hollywood rom-com, we would not advise you to use that part of our story as an example. Take it slow. There is nothing wrong with taking a few months or a year to really date, court, and get to know each other.

Every couple has to decide what it means for them to create a healthy foundation. As you can see from our story, we were two teenagers who had not fully worked through our trauma, and trying to create a relationship was not going to turn out well for us if we didn't stop and reevaluate what we were building together. We had to get serious about why we came to college and the purpose that we both wanted to have for our lives at the time. We had to start being firm with each other about getting to classes on time, staying focused, and then making time for each other after we took care of our priorities.

For you, that might mean taking a break in your relationship to work through your individual challenges. Or you might consider going to couples counseling together or setting up a weekly time to discuss what's going on in your personal lives so you can identify how your individual stressors are affecting your relationship. You can even give the time a special name. For some couples, you might have to decide that you don't have what it takes to create a healthy relationship, and that's all right, too. Creating a healthy foundation takes work, but the journey is worth it if you have someone who you can truly love out loud with.

3

Discovering the
Real You

As far back as our days in college, we've always been the couple who was moving light-years ahead of all of our friends. Everyone thought we were crazy back then, to be honest. We were the first ones to move out of Louisiana, buy our first house, and start the process of building our own family. But we had no way of knowing that moving to Atlanta would challenge both of us to examine how we saw ourselves individually as young gay Black men, how we wanted to create friendships, and how we wanted to show up in the world as a couple. We had more than a few fights in the beginning about who we wanted to be connected to and how we were going to navigate being in this new city together. In this chapter, we will take you into our adventure of discovering the real us as we bought our first home, navigated the difficulties of making and breaking our first chosen family, and learned how to sharpen our discernment along the way.

Jarius

When Terrell and I were juniors in college, we would often have "get-togethers" or game nights at our college apartment with a few of our friends. During one of these fun nights, I remember all of us talking about the future that we wanted for ourselves after graduation. That night, Terrell and I shared that we wanted to have three children and we even picked out their names: Ryan Anthony Joseph, Ashton Cole Joseph, and Aubrey Noelle Joseph. Now, if you're a true fan of ours, you'll know we used two of those names. This is important, so remember we told you ahead of time.

After our friends had left, Terrell and I continued talking about our future and we started thinking about where we wanted to live after graduation. While living in our off-campus apartments in college was more freeing for me than being in my hometown, I'd had enough of being looked at differently because of my sexuality. We initially ruled out Houston because moving there would seem like a typical move for someone from Louisiana. Moving to Houston would have been safe—I had visited Houston my entire life and many people followed the well-paved path from Louisiana to Texas and I didn't want any part of that. Not to mention Houston was hot as hell. We tossed out DC (too cold) and New York (too fast) as possibilities, too, and focused on finding a progressive city that would be conducive to our lives as gay Black men.

Atlanta kept moving to the top of our list because we believed that it would be a place where Black people were thriving and where we could have a lot of opportunity to grow in our careers and be open with who we were becoming. Atlanta also appeared to be a big progressive city with a thriving gay community (to be clear, Atlanta, not Georgia, because Georgia can be a hot mess toward our community). Terrell and I started digging deep into the housing market, and within a few months, we were only looking at homes in Atlanta.

During our senior year in February 2015, we took a trip to Atlanta. There, we found an advertisement for some new home builds we thought would be perfect. The day before we were supposed to leave, after enjoying a full weekend in Atlanta, we decided to go look at the model houses and we were instantly sold.

We ended up buying a three-story, 4,500-square-foot home with five bedrooms, three and a half bathrooms, and a movie theater. Both of us always held down a job, and Jarius even worked full-time during his junior year, and we also used our tuition reimbursement for a down payment along with our savings.

Walking through this gorgeous house, we truly felt like we had made it. We made this bold move to come to Atlanta without knowing another soul, and we were really thankful and grateful to have gotten through all the hurdles to make this moment happen. Everything in our lives was beginning to come into alignment. We'd signed a contract for a new build that would be ready in June, right after graduation—or so we thought.

When we went back to Atlanta in April, we were excited because we were promised that our new home would be finished in just two months. Much to our surprise, the developers updated us that the house would not be ready until October. Now we had to figure out what we were going to do.

But we didn't have enough time even to worry

because God worked the situation out in our favor. Funny enough, the model home that we originally toured was the house we ended up purchasing. We were able to move in on our original timeline in June of that year. We ended up spending the first five and a half years of our lives in Atlanta in that house. Being able to move into that house was a full circle moment for us and a true testimony of how God often works in mysterious ways in our lives.

Moving into that house at twenty-two years old felt like we had accomplished a huge goal that many only dream of. When we got the keys and we opened the door for the first time, I remember wanting to drop to my knees and just praise and thank God for opening up the door and blessing us with a significant accomplishment at such a young age; it felt like a huge blessing. We were grateful.

Terrell

Moving to Atlanta went hand in hand with how I felt moving away from home to Baton Rouge for the first time. It was another fresh start. But this time, I wasn't running headfirst from where I'd come from. This time, I believed that we were moving to a place where we saw people who looked like us.

For the first time, we saw Black people out and living as their true selves in Atlanta. I felt like this was going to be the start of Jarius and me being able to live as we truly were—a couple looking to start a family.

Was it scary moving to a new city? Hell yes. We were now leaving our safety net. Nobody was there to help us figure out closing costs or getting our first mortgage. Now, if something happened, we had to either drive at least ten hours to get home or figure it out ourselves.

Doing things on faith and figuring them out as we go speaks so much to how Jarius and I move through our relationship and how we navigate our lives. We couldn't tap into either one of our families for that kind of advice. We spearheaded it ourselves, and that's when I really started to see that building this new life was really going to be just me and Jarius. It was good to know that I had my person and that we were going to get through this thing called life together.

Now that we were homeowners, I want to keep it real with y'all. It wasn't all glitz and glamour. And while we made beautiful memories it was also us plunging into adulthood for real. I had to become the maintenance man, the lawn care specialist, and more. Jarius also lost his job during our first year as homeowners, which became a financial burden. We really leaned on each other during those times, and made the best out of every obstacle.

As we started settling into Atlanta, we became friends with a couple who were influencers before social media influencers became a big thing. They lived around the corner from us, so we started to slowly build a friendship with them, first saying hi when we saw one another outside, and eventually throwing whole dinner parties. This was one of the first Black gay couples to become prominent on social media. There were a few other couples who started doing their thing around the same time, but nobody had reached their level of success as far as we could see. They had a nice home, drove very nice cars, and had children—they were everything we aspired to be. As we hung out more, Atlanta started to feel like home.

We also knew a little bit about them before we moved to Atlanta, and one of the men in the couple wrote a book that actually inspired Terrell to eventually come out to his mom.

As we began to really seek out community, we became curious about whether or not our relationship values truly aligned with those of other couples in our new circle. As we mentioned, all of this was new to us and we were still learning what was the norm. There was one night in particular where we saw another couple coming out of a group dinner gathering and just before we got there, they gave us this stank look and we heard one of them say, "They must be up next." We had no idea what they were talking about in that moment, but we definitely knew spaces like that would be a no-go for us because we didn't play those catty games.

We've always been clear that we wanted to set a new standard for what a gay marriage could be and we certainly weren't open to anything like the lifestyle that we were beginning to see commonly in Atlanta. We began to have very serious conversations about what we were each willing to compromise on in regard to friendship and what we needed to feel whole and connected in our new city.

Jarius

Growing up, I witnessed my mom being so trusting of people and it always came back to bite her. Whether it was a family member or someone she was dating, people would end up stealing from her or using her insecurities to weaponize a situation against her. And guess who was there to pick up the pieces? Me! I had to wipe away her tears and tell her it was okay even though I was enraged and ready to fight anybody for hurting or disrespecting my mama.

After seeing my mother go through heartbreaking situations, I focused on keeping only good people around me—no fluff, no bullshit. I wanted good friendships and to celebrate good times with people I love. But as soon as I feel like someone or something is going to disrupt my internal peace, I decide not to put too much energy into it. At the same time, I know that having that kind of discernment can come off as me being judgmental or closed to meeting new people or not being open to new opportunities. Terrell has such an open heart and reminds me so much of my mom in that respect. He always wants to be the good person in a situation. But me? I don't have a problem flipping the truth switch and moving on to the next thing when a person's motives don't align with my values. It's a blessing and a curse.

During our first few years in Atlanta, there were huge lessons for me in learning to trust my discernment. As we started to expand our friend circle, I began to understand that it was important for me to have people around whose ideals and goals aligned with mine. Especially in marriage, I wanted Terrell and me to show up to events, gatherings, and work obligations as a united front.

As I began voicing this to Terrell, he would often say, "Jarius, you're being judgmental. Everyone's relationship is not going to look like ours!" This was where Terrell and I began to fundamentally disagree during our first few years in Atlanta. When he decides to be friends with someone, he goes all in. Because I know that people are human and I know that they will let you down, I've always felt like I needed to protect myself and Terrell from allowing people to take advantage of us. Now I know y'all probably thinking I'm a cutthroat type of person, but in reality it just takes a lot for people to earn my trust.

We had built up such a good relationship at that point that I didn't want outside influences to take away from what we were building. There was a certain amount of innocence coming from Louisiana, especially with it being a much smaller gay community, so there was still a lot for us to learn and I didn't want us to be taken off track.

When you move, especially to a larger city like Atlanta, one bad situation can eat you up and spit you out. We had to figure out what it means to be open with one another, and how to talk with our neighbors in the queer community. We had to realize that our awakening to being gay Black men and eventually our path to becoming parents would not be the same as everyone else's journey, gay or otherwise.

Lesson No. 5: It Takes Time to Discover the Real You

The biggest thing that we learned during our early years in Atlanta was that it really takes time to discover the real you—and we had to learn how to be patient with ourselves and each other as we grew, stumbled, and eventually got back up, only to keep falling and learning some more.

I'm sure that many of you have struggled with who you "should" be versus who you are or want to be. Maybe you're even like the two of us, raised to be people pleasers. But we can be so conditioned to please and match others that we suppress our own feelings and emotions to the point where our fears become greater than our dreams.

As you are growing and learning more about who you really are, it's natural to be conflicted about creating new friendships, expanding your inner circle, and changing your viewpoints about who you want to be. We have learned that you have to be cognizant and mature enough to be able to look at a situation and truly understand whether the outcome is likely to be good or bad.

We all deserve to be happy—and taking the time to discover who we are and how to get into alignment with what will make each and every one us of prouder of who we are will help us live out loud with a little more courage and grace each day.

4

Finding Grace
Through Grief

Creating the family of our dreams took a lot of work, prayer, and sacrifices. Once we were finally settled in Atlanta and had found our first dream home, we knew that we were now ready to pursue our desire to become fathers. But our road to becoming fathers was paved with our untraditional choice to embark on independent surrogacy and weathering the storm of losing our first child in a devastating miscarriage. Unfortunately there are still so many people who have challenged and questioned whether we should have become fathers in the first place. We still live in a world where people feel entitled to give their opinions about our desire to live our lives on our own terms. Through all of our ups and downs, we know that we have the right to declare that we deserve to have a family, too.

We started having conversations about becoming fathers while we were sophomores in college. We know that seems super early, but remember we told you that Terrell was super ambitious and him coming from a big family also played a factor in his wanting to get our family started right away. Also, the very thought of possibly being disowned once we came out was terrifying so we figured if we might lose our families for being gay, we needed to be prepared to build our own.

When we first began imagining what our family would look like, we dreamed about decorating nurseries for our children, having them in the best schools, building a safe environment where they could grow and thrive, and hopefully making it through the first few months without losing too much sleep. But being so young, we can now see how our naïveté could have led us right out of codependency to a new world of challenges. However, it was also our singlemindedness about what we wanted that reinforced our journey to becoming parents, even through intense loss. In this chapter, we will talk about the difficult road toward first-time fatherhood, our unexpected journey with grief, and how we learned to find the blessing on the other side of our heartbreak.

Jarius

In our relationship, Terrell has been the one who believes that we can do anything together. His ambition put us on an accelerated track to adulthood that included both of us taking on sales jobs where we were earning commissions while we were still undergraduates and living off campus in our first apartments. While we still enjoyed being young and living our lives, we knew that we were building a path that was far ahead of most of our friends and college peers around us. We were grateful that we were able to skip the normal challenges of wading through an entry-level job. Before we graduated, we were already saving up for what our potential parenting journey would be.

Thinking back, we missed out on a lot of the "typical" college experiences because we worked our asses off. We didn't get to go to football games, study sessions, or game nights on campus, etc. When we were not in school, we were mostly at work. Now, don't feel too bad for us—we knew how to suddenly fall ill with the best of 'em and take a sick day—but you get the point.

We both were very open about what type of fathers we wanted to be. We talked about everything from discipline to even vowing not to swear in front of the children. We knew it would be an uphill battle not having the world's acceptance, let alone our own families' acceptance, so we had to really be honest with each other about how life would be if it were just us and our kids. We really wanted to be intentional in all that we did with our future family. Our hope was that our children would always know how much we loved them and how much they were wanted.

But even with Terrell's ambition pushing us forward, I was very adamant about making sure that we had the right building blocks in place for our relationship to be successful. I wanted to make sure that we were moving forward into our relationship with a firm commitment of marriage and a solid home base. Before I knew it, shortly after the move, it was go time. We hadn't even gotten the boxes inside the front door before Terrell was researching and joining Facebook groups to learn more about how to find the right surrogate.

Within a few weeks, we found ourselves knee deep in conversations with other couples who had been through the surrogacy process. We discovered more about the advantages of going independent versus being matched with a surrogate via an agency. We were also researching surrogacy options outside of the country. While it was exciting to think through all these options, we also had our fears, too; at first, it felt incredibly overwhelming and scary. I was the one making sure that we were thinking things through rationally. Every day, we would sit and go through all the different options and see how much everything cost. In some surrogate situations, in particular when insurance does not fully cover the surrogate's health-care, the expectant parents would be required to pay for doctor's visits or to take care of any hospital expenses. But being married to someone who always believes that we can do the impossible made this process feel like we were going to find the perfect way to figure this out. But keep in mind we had just moved into a new house, furnished it, started new jobs, so where exactly were we going to get this money from?

Terrell

When we found our first surrogate, Jamilla, through an online surrogacy support group, it felt like we'd won the lottery. She lined up with everything that we were looking for at the time. She seemed like the answer to our prayers, and we were eager to move forward. We were immediately drawn to her quirky personality, Panamanian beauty, and friendly demeanor. She'd recently given birth to a son after having a difficult time getting pregnant, so she not only felt drawn to bless someone else with a child but also empathized with our desire to have our own family. Jamilla lived in Florida—a good five hours from us—but after a few calls with me, we were curious enough to drive down to meet her and her fiancé, Matt, at Chili's.

The vibe between the four of us seemed friendly enough to start, but that didn't last long. We tried to set the scene by telling them both to be honest and ask questions so that they would feel comfortable, but we were not prepared for what was about to come out of her fiancé's mouth. "So are y'all really gay? 'Cause y'all don't act gay or look gay!" I was stunned because no one had ever asked us that before. In his mind, he thought that we were two random Black guys trying to have a baby with his fiancé and that we were going to run off into the sunset as a throuple. Clearly we were gay but he just couldn't shake the feeling that we were hiding something. It was so awkward, and I noticed that Jarius was very turned off. Remember, Jarius was super overprotective, and he didn't want to see me get let down in the process. Jamilla also noticed how Jarius looked and quickly tried to excuse Matt's behavior. But I needed and wanted this to work, so I moved on and tried to steer the conversation in a positive direction. This was the first red flag that I ignored that would eventually come back and bite us.

Eventually, we agreed to come together and create this new life together. Jamilla was so excited to help our dream come true. A few weeks later, we agreed to meet with her and to use a home insemination kit while she was ovulating. We had been tracking her ovulation cycle with a kit, and when she got a smiley face, we jumped in our car for this five-hour drive and met up for the insemination. We did our part to provide our "sample," which I had been saving up for the past few days. We left the room and allowed her to do what she needed to do, only to be surprised with a call minutes later telling us she spilled it all trying to insert it. I felt like I had given my all, and my jaw dropped to the floor. We went to the local Wal-Mart to give me time to recharge, and, fortunately, we were able to give her another sample. We began to immediately pray for the best that this would work.

Within a few weeks, we were shocked to discover that our home insemination was successful on our first try! I was so excited that I wrote to the company who created the home insemination kit we used. They immediately responded and were so excited about our testimonial that it led to us being featured in a national article about infertility in the *Wall Street Journal*.

Now this was where things got interesting. In my excitement about our first pregnancy, I publicly shared on Facebook that Jarius and I were expecting our first child together—and at the same time, I officially came out and declared that I am gay. This was *huge* for me. I no longer wanted to hide or live in the shadows. I was now committed to live in my truth and to begin building our family on a firm foundation that did not include keeping our future child a secret. I couldn't be the amazing father that I wanted to be and still be afraid of who I was. It was scary and exciting at the same time to stand fully as the man who I always wanted to be.

While we had a lot of positive support and feedback from being featured in the *Wall Street Journal* article and were beginning to build our own community on social media, we had no way of preparing ourselves for some of the incredibly negative and hurtful feedback that came our way soon after. We'd been the only gay couple interviewed for the feature story, an article on the challenges of infertility, and for better or for worse, a ton of people wanted to let us know exactly what they thought about it.

Jarius and I were called everything but a child of God! There were more than a few people who were pissed that we were included in that article alongside heterosexual couples because those couples were somehow more disadvantaged than we were and our struggles to become parents were not the same. There were folks who questioned whether two men should be fathers to begin with. Those comments were incredibly demoralizing and soured our moment of celebration. And not to mention, it was completely unnecessary.

Lesson No. 6: Don't Let Your Dreams Make You Miss the Red Flags

While we were excited about finally being pregnant, we had no idea about the heartbreak we were going to face on the other side of our first pregnancy. We were on Cloud Nine and expecting our bundle of joy. But our excitement was immediately met with roadblocks and challenges. Once the money began rolling in, Jamilla and Matt quickly turned this beautiful situation into a strictly business arrangement.

More than once, Jamilla made it clear that she was juggling priorities—she was engaged, looking for a new job, balancing work and parenting, and trying to dig her way out of financial stress. So when updating us on her pregnancy started to fall off that list, we tried to be understanding. In our hearts, we knew Jamilla was doing the best she could, but we often felt left out. And feeling like we became dollar signs didn't sit well with us, either. Once we began to make our payments, the check-ins with Jamilla and Matt became few and far between. We only heard from them when a payment was soon due.

We were emotionally and financially invested, driving five hours to every doctor's appointment—and didn't even huff when she constantly rescheduled them. At this point what could we do? She was pregnant with our child, and she held all the power. When we'd show up, Jamilla acted inconvenienced, even a little resentful that we were both there. Finally, she made it clear that she didn't want to talk to us until it was time to give birth.

We felt so out of control but kept reminding ourselves that these were the cards we were dealt, since we didn't have $150,000 to work with a proper agency. So we rolled with the touch-and-go communication and walked on eggshells throughout her pregnancy. With all of our preparation, research, and dreaming, we had to ask, "How did we even get here?"

Terrell

Our relationship with Jamilla started off very genuinely. But you know what they say about hindsight. Still, it's worth a look back at what we missed that affected our pregnancy experience as surrogate fathers. We became so blinded by our desire to have a child that we missed make-or-break red flags. I can almost remember the night that I met Jamilla in a Facebook group. I'd spent hours researching how to find a surrogate, so that when she and I connected, my vision immediately shifted into "This has to work!" Even though she was the very first surrogate we'd gotten in contact with, we decided that she was going to be the one.

Soon, we found out that her partner, Matt, was jealous and unsupportive, and their relationship was unstable. Being so young, we thought that we could simply win him over. I remember saying to Jarius, "Let's just continue to build our plan and he will come on board. This is our only shot."

Even as we heard the horror stories from other couples on Facebook groups about surrogacy scamming, I was fiercely determined that that would not be us. We had just made so many big moves, and I was convinced that we were God's favorites and that we were invincible. So what could go wrong? As we soon discovered, everything could go wrong at any moment. We had to learn that just because you want something desperately doesn't mean that God won't have more than a few lessons for you to learn along the way. In choosing to overlook all of those red flags, maybe we shouldn't have been so surprised.

The Surprising Unraveling of Our Dream

Terrell

During a work trip in South Carolina, I received an alarming call. I had just finished a business dinner and was texting with Jarius on a shuttle back to my hotel when Matt's name showed up on my phone.

"The baby's gone," Matt said, his voice shaking. "The ambulance is on the way." I could hear Jamilla sobbing in the background. She was only five months along.

I immediately called Jarius and I couldn't even breathe. Jarius thought I was trapped in a car from a bad wreck, given the way I was hyperventilating. When I finally got the words out, he seemed relieved that I was okay and reassured me everything would be okay and that there had to have been a mistake. We had just seen our baby a few days prior at an ultrasound facility. She was jumping around in the womb and even waving at us. Clearly this was a mistake! But it was not.

While Jarius was driving, the hospital called me and explained what Matt hadn't: Jamilla had been having bad cramps and felt like she was having early contractions. While trying to push, her water broke, and that's when Matt called me. When Jamilla finally got to the ER, the doctor couldn't find our daughter Aubrey's heartbeat. He stayed on the phone as I was panicking on the other end. Eventually, the doctor had to hang up, leaving us devastated, with little to no information.

Then, a half hour later, the ER doctor called back to say that they'd found a heartbeat after all. *Was this doctor for real?* Though we didn't realize it at the time, our initial roller coaster was a sign of frustrating and unpredictable things to come.

When Jarius got to the hospital, everything seemed calm enough. But after being thrust onto an emotional roller coaster, I couldn't think straight. I checked out of my hotel the next day, after having to sit through a six-hour conference when all I wanted to do was get to my baby. I felt backed into a corner because while I had come out on social media to family and friends, my coworkers didn't know I was gay, much less expecting a child! The conference included all the company's executives and I started to worry that if I left and they found out about my sexuality, that would be the end of my career, because you never know how people feel. Imagine being on the verge of losing a child, but because of societal expectations, I had to weigh out all of those considerations at the same time. Once I was able to leave, I was so scattered that it's a miracle that I made it to Florida in one piece.

Jamilla was experiencing what's known as a "premature rupture," which prompts many hospitals to keep the mom in the hospital until the baby is born. Usually, the parent is put on bed rest, given steroids to help the baby's lungs grow quickly, given antibiotics to help prevent infection in the mom and child, and monitored very closely in a hospital setting until the infant's lungs have grown enough to induce labor.

Our doctor sent Jamilla home to rest, elevate her legs, and drink lots of fluids. The doctor said there was a chance the baby would survive if she did this. We didn't agree with this decision, but they gave us no choice. We went into battle mode and bought more fluids than you'd need to hydrate a football team. Even so, I had a bad feeling about not leaving Jamilla at the hospital. I quickly found another hospital an hour away and insisted that we all pile into the car and demand to be seen.

Although Jamilla and Matt hated this idea—they

felt we were being overly cautious and controlling, and she simply wanted to rest—I got us to the hospital, where we begged a nurse to admit Jamilla. She insisted that although Jamilla was at 19 weeks and 6 days, the hospital couldn't help the baby at fewer than 20 weeks. *We were only 24 hours away from this milestone!*

I began to cry and I was pleading with the admitting nurse to make an exception. After seeing me break down, she reluctantly agreed to admit us. Isn't it funny how so much power rests in the hands of a compassionate person? That was our first hurdle to overcome, and we started to feel more hopeful.

Once Jamilla was admitted, the doctor agreed to do an ultrasound. However, he bluntly insisted that no matter his findings, there was likely nothing they could do to save the baby, since her lungs wouldn't be developed enough to use a breathing tube for artificial breathing. He basically implied that our daughter would likely die.

Only Matt was allowed to stay in the hospital room for Jamilla's initial ultrasound—even though *we* were the baby's expectant parents. Now the door was literally being shut on us. We had to wait to hear for an update before the doctor came out.

On the scan, the doctor saw that Aubrey had already made her way down the birth canal. Thank God I had insisted on checking into a second hospital. At this point, there was no way to stop Aubrey from pushing her way into the world. All we could do was pray that she'd somehow figure out how to breathe on her own. To make matters worse, our doctors and nurses hardly acknowledged us and insisted we wait *outside the delivery room* while our daughter was delivered. Matt, of course, was allowed to stay with Jamilla. This hospital treated us like fourth cousins or, even worse, social pariahs.

Waiting outside the room, it felt like we had no air to breathe. So we decided to take a walk. Somehow we ended up driving to a nearby AutoZone, where we just sat in the parking lot. Neither one of us spoke to the other. We just sat in silence, with tears rolling down our faces and our minds racing a million miles per hour. We didn't know what to do. In that moment, I remember feeling cheated. *Why is this happening to us?* I began questioning my faith after feeling like we were so blessed in our prior accomplishments. How could this be our reality?

Jarius

To be honest, I wanted to pack it in and go home. On the one hand, we remained hopeful, but we also weren't naïve. We knew what we were up against, and I didn't want to deal. It was Terrell who insisted we see this puzzling situation through to its very end—whatever that would be. During the worst day of our lives, we only had each other—and it had to be enough.

Eventually we got the call to say that active labor had begun and we needed to head back to the hospital. I was so afraid. I was terrified to see what we had worked so hard for come crashing down. Once we got back to the hospital, we stood in front of the door and I began to pray. I was begging God to somehow deliver a miracle in this situation for us. A few short moments later, the door opened, and we could see Jamilla and Matt both crying. Jamilla only had to push twice, and Aubrey was out. Because Aubrey was so small and had no protection inside the womb, her journey through the birth canal damaged her body. The nurses brought her over to an incubator and placed Aubrey under a heat lamp. Her appearance was startling at first but still somehow beautiful—though her head was misshapen, she had long eyelashes and tufts of soft hair on her head. Terrell rubbed her little belly and toes to let her know she was loved as he wept over her. In that moment, I went back into protection mode and sucked up my feelings to be there for Terrell. His whole world was crashing down. I didn't want him to feel hurt and broken. I did my best to soothe him and let him know that everything would be okay.

Aubrey had passed before she was born. Because Jamilla was one day shy of the 20-week mark, the hospital called her passing a miscarriage—but she looked and felt like a stillborn. We cried our eyes out and were only given ten minutes to work through our feelings and say goodbye. The whole experience felt so disorienting.

Who knew pregnancy could take such a drastic turn so quickly? A business-as-usual nurse asked if we wanted Aubrey cremated or shipped to Georgia for a funeral. I couldn't believe that they were so quick to go through the motions and not allow us to be human and have that moment. I resented her for that. We made a quick decision to have Aubrey cremated and sent back home to us. The next thing you know, they took her away.

Matt and Jamilla cried, too, as we awkwardly hugged them goodbye. The rest of the day was a blur. We each walked to our cars, feeling like zombies. I don't even remember coming down the elevator. I felt so numb that I didn't recall seeing anyone around me or even walking outside the hospital doors. I don't even know how I ended up at my car door.

We couldn't drive home together since we'd driven

separately. We didn't even talk on the phone. We felt so, so alone and the sadness became about more than the loss itself. All of Terrell's cousins were pregnant and delivering babies with no problem around the same time, and here we were the only ones who fell short. *Why was this happening to us? Why didn't God have our backs?*

When we got home, we returned to a deafening quiet. Somehow our new home felt too big and too empty. We glanced into what was meant to be Aubrey's room—crammed with a crib, car seats, baby clothes, and other infant necessities in and out of boxes. As expectant fathers, we felt like we'd just ridden a broken, emotional roller coaster. It was one of our biggest dreams to become dads and give Aubrey a loving and limitless childhood. We'd prepared our house and hearts for Aubrey for months. We were at our highest, most thrilling point when we found out we were expecting, and then *whoosh*—we crashed down when we lost her. We were tempted to close her bedroom door forever, maybe even barricade it with yellow police tape until we were ready to revisit fatherhood again. We felt surrounded by total darkness, with no light to guide us back out into the world.

Now what?

Lesson No. 7: Finding
Grace Through Grief

Terrell

We learned to face our fears…by simply facing them. There's no other way to manage pain that's in front of you. And once you do, you build strength for the next time that you must face a challenge or a trauma. Believe it or not, every time you rise, you get stronger. Ideally, your mind will eventually learn that life is full of these experiences, and you will feel less afraid of them each time.

We also wish we would have been warned about the emotional toll that a pregnancy can take on fathers. We both went into our first surrogacy thinking that every pregnancy would be successful, and once you get pregnant, that's it. This is the kind of stuff that would have been great to learn about in school instead of fractions and all that other bull crap that we don't use or even remember. It would've been nice to know that pregnancies can come with the possibility of miscarriages, gestational diabetes, or high blood pressure, and the high mortality rates for mothers in the Black community.

My mother had a miscarriage when I was in elementary school, and being so young at the time, I didn't understand what was going on. I remember the whispers around the house and in our family that she had lost a baby. Obviously because I was a child, no one explained it to me. But I just think back to that time of what my mother might've felt or how lonely she could've been by not being able to share that out loud with anyone, not even with her children. I only learned about this as an adult, and even when my mother and I talked about it, I could tell it was something she wasn't super comfortable discussing. For my mother, for us, and for every person who has gone through grief in their parenting journey, I wish that we had all been more equipped to know that a pregnancy can go so many different ways, and not just the way that you want it to go.

Jarius

As difficult as it was, we had to learn how to start communicating, however imperfect it was at the time. We also found incredible support through online communities. We didn't see a lot of gay Black couples going through this journey, and we weren't sure there were any at all, given the reception to our *Wall Street Journal* feature.

As we grieved, we openly communicated our raw

emotions and shared how we felt, as we felt it. We each created a safe space for the other person to fully process and share his feelings. We listened and gave each other the room to feel whatever we felt. We picked each other up when the other person needed it and vowed to see each other through.

A few weeks after we lost Aubrey, the mood in our home shifted. We lay in bed, goofing around for the first time in a while, and I remember Terrell cracking his first smile. I don't even remember what was so funny—but the joke wasn't the point. What mattered was that we were on the path to being us again. It may sound spontaneous, but without making the decision to lean into one another in those first days of grief, we would have drifted apart completely. In this moment of laughter, we recognized ourselves, our relationship, and our hope for becoming parents in a new light. This made me so happy that I insisted on taking a photo to capture the moment. It was 1:30 a.m., and I was beaming while Terrell's face was all squished up, pushing out his best grin. This was what our future looked like. This was the start of knowing that our relationship would be okay. We weren't giving up yet.

As you move through difficult moments in your

own life, we hope that you can learn from our story and know that nothing is impossible. Even if your communication in the beginning is awkward, tough, and filled with uncertainty, it's more than okay to keep trying when you're with someone you love and who you know is sharing the same dreams.

Lesson No. 8: You Have to Release the Wheel

Surrogacy has humbled us in the most gut-wrenching yet most loving ways. There are no words that can be said about losing a child. Something leaves your body and soul, and a piece of you is gone. All the hopes and dreams we had for her, the late-night conversations we had, laughing and wondering what she would be like, the anticipation and excitement to see her face, were just gone in an instant. We felt powerless and knew that if there were anything we could give to get her back, it would have been done in a heartbeat.

We'd never even considered miscarriage as a possibility; we'd thought that 20 weeks meant we were safe and able to celebrate. But our first surrogacy experience scarred us so that we could essentially never be that happy again—and that hurts. We have never allowed ourselves to have that much joy because of the fear that it'll get ripped away again. As a result, we turned into overly cautious parents.

On the back end, we now recognize that one of those red flags that we missed was understanding the emotional trauma that a pregnancy could have for a surrogate—and for us. We discovered later on just how much turmoil our pregnancy was causing between Jamilla and her fiancé. And while she might have been able to move forward from this devastating loss, our entire world fell apart. We wish that there had been a little bit more compassion toward us. Crazy enough, while she was the one who was carrying the child, we felt that we were more connected to our daughter.

Since we were building up our social media presence, we took the time to make a long and thoughtful post about losing Aubrey. But it was super tough because not everybody sees everything on social media at the same time. We would periodically get DMs asking us, "Is she still pregnant?" or "When is she due?" It was incredibly difficult for us to hold on to our hope while managing everyone else's expectations. But even with having to write back those uncomfortable and sometimes difficult responses, we still felt joy in knowing that we were building this community that, over time, we would learn to lean on. Up until that point, there were no public families that looked like ours that we could look up to, so we hoped to fill a niche and help others like us. We began to feel comfort with these complete strangers that we were not able to find within our own families and communities.

We never want to steal the joy of parenthood from anyone, but we have learned that you have to truly release the wheel. Of course, you want to make sure that you are doing all of your research and being involved as much as you can in every step of the process. But then you have to come to a point in your journey where you realize that nothing can prepare you for what to expect along your path. No two parenting journeys are the same. You do your best to make the wisest decisions and then you have to trust that you and your partner will have the strength, courage, and faith to take on whatever comes along with your experience.

We also wish that we had been more equipped to handle our pregnancy experiences with our surrogates because each pregnancy can go so many different ways. You have to have a strong support system. While we were glad to have each other during each of our surrogacies, in truth, you will need more support than just your spouse. With our first pregnancy, we were super excited and openly shared our experiences on social media. Even though we appreciated and were grateful for that virtual support from our online communities, we still needed in-person support because we had no idea what to expect.

5

Building the Faith Muscles You Never Knew You Needed

We put everything we had—money, heart, even the strength of our relationship—into creating our family. It changed us to know that we are all we have. As young parents, we learned so much about how important it is to do things for the right reason and discover what was genuine to us. We'd finally built our dream family. We had our own little clan, and no matter how our families felt, this would be our constant and the family we'd created would be our home.

The decision to start our parenting journey back up was not easily made. Jarius had to be Terrell's rock, so he didn't have the opportunity to grieve the loss of our daughter himself. Instead, he naturally fell into a problem-solving role, wanting to hurry up and get us back on the path, not understanding at the time that people grieve differently. While Jarius was ready to get back to the fatherhood journey almost immediately, Terrell was reluctant, because it felt like to him that we were replacing Aubrey.

Three months later, we decided to move forward and try again. We went through a plethora of uncomfortable situations that ranged from considering adoption, which almost led us into a scam, to an in-home surrogate, who we thought ran off with our baby after conception.

In this chapter, we will explore the challenges of becoming first-time fathers, learning to be the best advocates for our children, and discovering the rewards on the other side of grief and heartbreak.

Terrell

Here we are after the miscarriage, with thousands of dollars in baby items, a crib, and a room ready to have another child. We felt like we were back at square one, not knowing if our luck would pan out the same way. We just knew our lives were incomplete without a baby.

The biggest thing we had to get out of our minds was the fear of suffering another miscarriage, so we considered adoption. This decision was based on the baby already being born, not having to wait nine months, and avoiding the possibility of anything going wrong. We switched gears from surrogacy groups to adoption groups. We found a woman who was local, had just given birth, and was looking for an adoptive family. We were just twenty-three at the time and had no idea how this process worked or what we were doing.

We began texting back and forth with her, and she told us more about the baby. She shared with us that the baby had already been born, and the father was not involved. The baby was a secret and she wanted to find the right family to pair the baby with.

She had found us on Facebook and—much to our surprise— had already gone through our social media profiles and status. During one of our first calls, she noted that she didn't like one of the statuses that Jarius had written, and I immediately got mad with him and said, "You are ruining this for us!"

Jarius cleaned up his page, and she agreed to move

forward with us. We set a date to meet at a local park. Now, everything we'd been taught about stranger danger went straight out the window. Our parents would have been so disappointed in us. No one knew where we were going or who we were meeting.

When we met her in person, we saw that she was a heavy-set white woman. She seemed normal and even-keeled. However, throughout our conversation we were on high alert and checked our surroundings every few minutes. She told us she needed to run home and that she would give us a call later that night so we could meet the baby at the hospital.

But the call never came.

A few hours later, I went to the hospital, where she told us she would be, and I asked for her status in the maternity ward. The person at the front desk said that they had no record of her. I felt the air leave my body— we were back in limbo once again.

When we didn't hear back from her, we put the pieces together and figured out that there never had been a baby and that she'd been scamming us. Oddly enough, she didn't want money; we believe she wanted attention and sympathy. This is when we learned what an "emotional scammer" is. The experience broke us down even more.

Jarius

After the adoption fiasco, when most would have given up, we were determined to reach our goal. Our spirits were broken but we kept our eyes on the light at the end of the tunnel. We went back to what we knew from the surrogacy world because obviously adoption wasn't it for us.

We matched with a young lesbian woman in South Carolina who already had a young son. She had a very similar story to Jamilla's, as she said she wanted to bless another same-sex family with a child. At first, everything seemed perfect, but her girlfriend was skeptical about the process. This time we were very proactive about getting a better understanding of the girlfriend's concerns. She was up and down. Some days she was supportive and others she wasn't. We knew that if the surrogate didn't have a good support system, it wouldn't work out.

We drove back and forth to South Carolina for our insemination attempts. And then one day we got a call that she and her girlfriend were breaking up. She asked us if she could move in. This wasn't ideal, but what could we do? Her only other option was to move back with her family on the West Coast, and we didn't want her to be that far away from us.

We allowed her to move in with her son and make herself right at home. But, yet again, here we were, ignoring all the red flags. Soon after she moved in, she started to bring women over for overnight dates. We didn't have any issues with her having her own life and dating, but I'm not one for waking up and seeing a stranger in my house first thing in the morning. It just goes to show the lengths that we were willing to go to have kids.

Needless to say, this was another situation that didn't work out. Her family had put so much religious guilt on her that she began feeling "wrong" for having a baby for us. They convinced her to come home, and she left right after we inseminated. We begged and pleaded with her, but we couldn't exactly force her to stay (otherwise that would be kidnapping!). Her mind was made up, and we had to let her go without being 100 percent sure if she was pregnant or not. Once she moved back home, we monitored her social media closely and discovered that she wasn't pregnant after all. We still didn't have the baby that we wanted.

Within a few weeks we were back on the surrogacy boards and began matching again with prospective surrogates. This time, instead of leaving our hopes and dreams up to one surrogate, we were talking to multiple people. One of the first prospective mothers that we connected with was Tina. This was perfect because Tina was in Georgia. No more five-hour drives each way, and we could be more involved throughout the entire process. However, after several attempts, Tina was not getting pregnant. This was hard for all of us, as we really wanted to make it work, but we knew that we would eventually have to move on.

But like we told you, we were talking with multiple surrogates. Our next match was with a woman named Amber who lived in Michigan. We flew to Michigan and did an insemination attempt with Amber, and within two weeks she got pregnant on the first try.

AND THEN—a few weeks later, we got a surprise call from Tina that she was pregnant, too!

We were so elated to be expecting two babies at the same time. Terrell had always wanted twins, so this was quite a serendipitous way for our babies to come into our lives. While it was a happy moment, we were still scared. We were definitely leaning on our faith and praying harder than we ever had before. We were mentally preparing ourselves for anything and everything. While we felt more confident this time, we still didn't tell anyone what was happening.

The day Tina went into labor, we had talked with her that afternoon and told her she could call us at any time as soon as she began feeling contractions. Little did we know that we were going to get a call from her that night telling us that she needed us to pick her up immediately and that it was go time.

Once we checked into the hospital, the doctor reassured us that she was just having Braxton-Hicks contractions and that she was not going into labor yet. But as he checked her cervix, her water broke. Jarius was in the delivery room, and Terrell was anxiously standing by in the waiting room when our son, Ashton, was born on July 27, 2017—and our dreams to become fathers finally came true.

Now, if you've been keeping up, you know that nothing has ever been easy for us. When Ashton was born weighing just three pounds and eleven ounces, we were taken aback. We had been to every appointment, and there were no signs of anything being wrong during his development. He was diagnosed with IUGR, and our hearts immediately melted to the floor. All the doctors could tell us was that there weren't any guarantees on how Ashton would do, and that if he did make it, we had a long road ahead of us. Much to our joy and delight, Ashton exceeded all expectations that the doctors had for his development. He was hitting growth and development milestones faster than expected and we were anxious to become a family outside of these hospital walls. After almost two weeks in the hospital, we got the word that we were cleared to take our son home.

Those first few days of fatherhood felt surreal. This dream that we had been talking about, wishing, and praying for was finally here. We were very grateful but at the same time incredibly nervous. This baby was really ours now and we had to do this thing called fatherhood on our own. We felt like we were on an emotional seesaw, complete joy of parenting on one side and constant anxiety and prayers that we were doing everything right on the other. Within a matter of days, we went from having four weeks left to prepare for Ashton's arrival to now being catapulted into a new routine of caring for this precious life.

Terrell

Ashton was in the NICU for nearly two weeks. Much longer than anyone would have liked, but long enough to build some sense of comfort and routine with the twenty-four-hour hospital staff monitoring him. But even with that constant care, we were still on high alert.

There wasn't anything in this world Jarius and I wouldn't do to love and care for this baby, but in reality we knew we wouldn't be able to bring him home without the help of the doctors and nurses. So the feeling of fatherhood didn't fully kick in for us for a while. Our care team was cautious about not giving us a false sense of hope, so we didn't know that we were free to go home until the day before Ashton was cleared.

After our hospital team had assured us that Ashton could breathe, eat, and be with us on his own, we felt an overwhelming sense of relief. However, once we'd put this tiny baby into his car seat—we were hit with the stark realization that our work was just beginning. We will never forget sitting in the parking lot of the hospital and just thanking God for seeing us through this time. This was a feeling we knew all too well, but now we had gotten our happy ending.

During those first few days we handled him like a piece of glass. Every time he moved or stirred we were both incredibly alert to make sure that he was good. Initially Jarius wanted to practice co-sleeping to promote bonding, but we both agreed that it would be best for him to learn how to sleep on his own. Fortunately, Ashton was a good sleeper. But that didn't stop us from constantly checking on him to make sure that he was still breathing. Listen, we'd given so much of ourselves to get this child here, so there was no way in hell we were going to let something happen on our watch. When Ashton was born, no one knew that he had arrived. We weren't comfortable bringing people into our journey just yet. We were in full nesting mode.

Three weeks later, we were just beginning to feel settled after finally getting Ashton home from the NICU, and getting the hang of becoming fathers, when we got a call from Amber saying that she'd fallen down a flight of stairs and was going into labor. We were like, "C'mon, God!" As you can imagine, our world came crashing down yet again! The bliss we had been experiencing was taken from us, and we went back into fighting mode to make sure our daughter Aria was okay.

We now had to figure out how to get to our surrogate and our daughter as soon as possible *and* take care of a newborn at home. We didn't want to risk bringing Ashton on a plane at less than two months old—we do not play with germs. Eventually, we decided that I would go to be with our surrogate and Jarius would stay home.

As soon as I left, my anxiety went through the roof. I couldn't control things from hundreds of miles away, and there was no guarantee that things would go according to our plans. *What if I don't get there on time? What if the surrogate forgets our hospital plan? Will our lawyer get to the hospital in time?* (We'd gone through more official means this time around.) *What if our surrogate gave birth and started bonding with our baby without us? What if she's changed her mind and wants to keep her?*

Jarius

When I think about Aria's personality now and how she came into the world, I realize she has always been a girl who does exactly what she wants. But when she was on the way, I didn't know what to expect. Nothing in any of our pregnancies had ever gone as planned.

Fortunately, we lived close to the airport in Atlanta and Terrell was able to fly out fairly quickly to reach our surrogate in Michigan. He got to our surrogate's hospital a few hours after the birth. Aria was born healthy on September 2, 2017—with no grueling and scary NICU process this time around. Once Terrell came back home to Atlanta with her, I thought we could finally be at peace as a family. We were super grateful to both of our surrogates for bringing our kids into the world. We'd had our fair share of bills, family drama, and scary situations, but they were indeed part of our fatherhood journey. Little did we know that our surrogates would stick around a little while longer.

In most surrogacy setups, there's a window of time when a surrogate can potentially change her mind about wanting to keep the child and file for parental rights. Although all of our children are biologically ours, the second-parent adoption process for same-sex couples can be incredibly tough. Because we went with a traditional surrogacy route, the surrogates were also the biological mother. So we had to obtain an official surrender from each of our surrogates to give up their parental rights, which would then remove them from the respective birth certificate. This would allow the second father to legally adopt so that we both could be recognized as parents.

For Ashton and Aria, we had to wait three weeks after each of their births before we could officially move forward with the adoption process. For some couples, depending on the state where their child is born, that wait can be as long as three months!

It felt like we were barely breathing during that time, and the end felt so far away. We still had to assume responsibility for our kids, but there was always this fear in the back of our minds that something could go left because family courts don't traditionally favor fathers. However, we were soaking up every moment and living out our dreams as fathers.

So we found ourselves in a bind when both of our surrogates started making crazy requests after the births. One of our surrogates asked us to pay her car note and the other surrogate wanted us to give her a very expensive pair of designer shoes as her "push gift."

At the time, I was like, "Girl, are you kidding me?!" I was getting only 80 percent of my pay from my job because I was out on paternity leave. We had two newborn children at home, we were paying for donor breastmilk for both of them, and on top of that, I had to worry about our surrogates' bills and Balenciagas? Child, it was way too much.

Still, Terrell and I couldn't risk saying no and pissing either one of them off. I now know that neither one of our surrogates had any ill intentions and they really wanted to do the right thing by me and Terrell. But when you're sleep deprived and your anxiety is through the roof, you will do anything to protect your child. We'd worked way too hard to become fathers, and we weren't gonna let a car payment or an overpriced pair of shoes stand in the way of us having our family.

Terrell

Second-parent adoption is a highly involved process with background checks and costs that we weren't prepared for. For Jarius and me to adopt Ashton and Aria respectively, the courts had to send someone to our home to make sure that that our house was safe for our children. We each had to have character references, verify our income, and take mental tests to make sure we were "fit" to be parents. It felt like we were being targeted. We had done everything we were "supposed" to do, but with every step I kept wondering *Why are we in a situation where we have to prove how much money we have just to show that we want to have a child?*

It felt like a never-ending cycle—surrogate problems, birth problems, health problems, adoption problems. We were constantly chasing a finish line. It was almost like we were begging someone to validate us as parents. I remember at the time I kept saying, "How much more do we have to do to prove that we are worthy of having our kids?"

But because we're a same-sex couple, we get asked all these extra questions about our motivations for parenthood on top of the standard barrage of questions about income and our ability to take care of our kids. It feels like we always have to constantly prove that we deserve our children and that we're good parents—and that's hard.

We had to unlearn everything that we had ever been taught about becoming parents, because those lessons had come from couples who were both biological parents. They don't have safety checks for their homes or their mental capacity. So now we had to create a new blueprint for what our fatherhood journey would be.

Becoming a Party of Five

Terrell

Jarius and I were so young when we had Ashton and Aria. But when we decided to have our third child, our daughter, Aspen, we felt that we were in a better place to add to our family. We had learned from our previous surrogacies and were confident that things were going to be different this time around. We both had baby fever and were excited for all the milestones like a gender reveal party and a baby shower.

Fortunately, when it came time to choose a surrogate for Aspen, we had already known our fourth surrogate, Nicole, for seven years. I met her in a Facebook surrogacy group right after losing our first daughter. Facebook groups for expectant parents are mostly an open place for people to ask questions and form genuine community, but like many social media forums, group members can get wild real fast, and become quick to impose their standards on others. I remember asking a simple question and there were women in one of these groups who were jumping all over me for just trying to get more information. Nicole was quick to come to my defense and set the folks in that group straight. She immediately asked these people, "Why are y'all acting so crazy? He's just asking a question!"

From there, we stayed in touch with Nicole over the years. We would connect on FaceTime every so often and she kept us in the loop about the birth of her son and her surrogacy journey of giving birth to twins for a couple. She would always say, "I'm gonna be your surrogate one day, so just let me know when you are ready."

When we were ready to move forward and get serious about adding to our family, we did all the required background checks and made sure that our attorney drew up the right paperwork. This time we went in with lots of thought and intention to make the most of the experience. Nicole knew about our past journeys, so it was her goal to make sure that we enjoyed this process, too.

But at just five months into her pregnancy, Nicole's blood pressure began to spike, and as a result, the doctors thought that our baby was going to have a hard time growing. The further she got into her pregnancy, the clearer it became that her blood pressure was getting higher and higher. The doctors recommended that she deliver the baby early. Now here we were again, facing another premature birth and having to make incredibly hard decisions about how to move forward as fathers. While we were initially expecting our daughter to come in early summer, she was now on her way at the end of March.

We welcomed our third child, Aspen, on March 25, 2023, and she was born weighing only two pounds and seven ounces. She was our smallest baby yet, and born across the country, which had not been the plan.

Jarius

Everything in our life at that moment was new. We were engulfed in our parenting life *and* our professional life. We had opened up a restaurant a month before Aspen was born, we were still working on content for social media, and we still had deliverables due for all of our sponsors. We had to smile on camera and make good on all these commitments while we were going through the toughest part of our lives.

Thankfully, we had an understanding management team who kept our content crisp and clean. Still, most of our brand partners didn't know what was going on. But our fear was that if we said we needed more time, how were we going to continue making money to take care of our family or fly back and forth across the country to take care of Aspen while footing the bill for her NICU stay?

We were high on a lot of emotions and then all of our stress got piled even higher when we discovered that Aspen was having stomach issues when she was first born. Terrell kept bringing up the fact that he saw that her stomach was not quite right. She was so tiny and her stomach was swollen. The more we brought it up to the doctors, the more certain they seemed to be that it was gas that would go away.

Then, the morning we were to be discharged from the NICU, we got a call at telling us that Aspen was being rushed to the OR for emergency surgery. With no additional information, we felt incredibly scared that they weren't telling us the truth.

After the surgery, we started flying back and forth across the country to spend time with Aspen and Ashton and Aria equally. The time difference was killing us. It was back and forth between red-eyes and early morning flights. We just couldn't keep going nonstop like this. I knew that we weren't being the parents we could be because we were stretched so thin.

We felt so much guilt for not being able to be there with Aspen 24/7. I couldn't escape the feeling of thinking that our child was going through so much in the NICU and she was all by herself. Of course, the staff and the nurses were going to take care of her, but there's nothing like a parent's love. I just wanted to be there to hold her and reassure her that she was going to get through it.

Lesson No. 9: The Tough but Necessary Faith Workout

Jarius

After our NICU experience with Aspen, I learned that I don't need to be blindly following anybody in this life, aside from God. While we trusted that the doctors and everyone in a hospital had the best of intentions and years of medical training, at the end of the day, everybody is human. Doctors sometimes work six days a week, twelve hours a day, without being able to go home and see their own families. So how do you think they feel at the end of the day? They're not perfect and nobody's going to advocate for your child the way you can as a parent.

I'm glad that Terrell's discernment kicked in and said, "Nah, something ain't right with our daughter." When we listened to it, sure enough, we knew we had to kick into high gear. One of our other blessings during that time was that we were able to talk with Ashton's former nurse in the NICU. She helped us put on our suits of armor. I remember her telling us,

"This is your child, and you have to be an advocate for her. Even though she's in the NICU with round-the-clock care, you have to stay on everyone's asses. Even when people are super sweet, do what you have to do to because no one's gonna do it for you like you will." When she said that, it was almost confirmation for us to make sure that Aspen had the best care.

Terrell

Getting to the other side of grief and ultimately being able to become a family was like getting through a tough but necessary workout. You know how you just hate working out and going to the gym? It's necessary if you want to be healthy and have the kind of body that you want, but you just hate it. You feel sore and exhausted, but at the end of the day, you always feel better, and you feel good about yourself when you get the results that you want. You know ultimately that it's going to be worth it.

We spent fifty days in the NICU with Aspen, and we were absolutely miserable during most of that time. But once we had the all clear to take her home, we got on the first red-eye back to Atlanta, and we realized that there was nothing that we wanted more than to add this new little baby to our family. All that pain was just a drop in the bucket compared to the joy that we feel now.

Jarius

We can see now that God was flexing and working our faith muscles. When each of our kids was born, it felt the hardest right after they came home. But then as the months continued, it got progressively easier and easier. Eventually, when we had a little time to just sit back and enjoy being fathers, I could finally settle into the moment and say, "Oh my God, how blessed are we?"

I am extremely grateful to have my relationship with my husband, enjoy my children, and be on a good path with my career. We really aim to cherish every part of the journey with our kids because we know that tomorrow isn't promised. Who knows what kind of parents we would be if we hadn't lost our first child? Who knows if we would have the same kind of patience and care with our children had we not gone through the stress of dealing with our surrogates or praying our kids through the NICU?

When I look back to how hard it was in 2016 when we lost Aubrey, it sucked. But I believe what got us through was looking forward to when God would bring us to the other side of it. I've learned to have the kind of faith in God to know that he'll open doors even farther than what I could imagine or think of.

Lesson No. 10: It's Okay to Face Your Trauma

As we both reflect back on our fatherhood journey, we both wish that we had taken more time to deal with and process our childhood traumas before becoming parents. It feels good that we can trust each other to be great co-parents and to walk through the expected and unexpected challenges of parenthood together. But unfortunately, we know that many couples are in the thick of raising their children without a good spouse or partner to lean on. Additionally, if you're not healed within yourself, we don't know how on earth you can consciously raise a child to be a sound and well-rounded human being.

Jarius also wishes that he would have done more to heal his relationship with his family. He grew up in a family that lacked emotional support and focused on a lot of nitpicking and fussing. He had to think long and hard about, *Do I want to transfer these kinds of behaviors to my child?* It's things like this, which you might not even know about, that you have to work through.

Also, for us both growing up in the Black community, there's so much residual trauma that Black people specifically carry. Especially when it comes to anger. If we don't work that out before we have children, we will pass it on to them and wonder why they act the way they do.

We both can be very critical of ourselves as parents. There's always room for improvement, and it's very easy to settle into what you've always known. Even though we give ourselves grace, we can't just say, "We didn't get it right today, so we're not going to try again tomorrow." When you have kids, that's not enough. Our children didn't ask to be brought into the world, and they didn't ask to be part of our family. So we do our absolute best to give them our best.

We've learned that you really can't have expectations when you have children. You learn as you go, and after a while, something just clicks. For us, we are grateful that we have learned how to be great co-parents with each other, and to take the time to really process and bounce ideas off each other. This is not to say that people can't do it by themselves. But it definitely is beneficial to have a co-parent who is on the same page.

6

Becoming the Representation That We Wanted to See

After we moved to Atlanta and officially became parents, Terrell was doing marketing and sales for Stanley Black & Decker, and Jarius was working in a traditional sales role with ADP. Social media was the first business that we ran together. We've always dabbled in the same industries and same companies, but working together was a totally new experience for us. Now we were in charge. In those early days, our path in social media was just figuring it out as we went. The more we posted, the more people we started to reach. We were excited to put more of our energy into building the community that we always dreamed of having, making our voices heard, and creating a legacy that we could be proud of.

In this chapter, we will explore how we began building a new path for ourselves on social media, how we balanced perceptions with reality, and how we ultimately learned how to do this thing we love while prioritizing our peace.

Jarius

I started the Terrell and Jarius profile on Instagram, and Terrell started T & J Family on YouTube. When we began posting on social media, there were no other Black gay male couples who looked like us or represented the things we stood for online. Every couple that we saw was white, and often they were much older than us. This made sense because, typically, older, more affluent people are the ones who can afford surrogacy and adoption. In our opinion, they often face less resistance to achieving those goals. But we needed to see people who looked like us, spoke like us, and had the experiences we had. Honestly, it felt unfair.

Eventually we said to ourselves, "We're not going to

live in the shadows or hide our children. Let's be the representation that we're looking for."

For me, when we first started, I was all about changing the narrative of what Black gay love looks like online. We started out by posting updates about our first baby with our first surrogate in January 2016. That led to the *Wall Street Journal* article that tore us up about wanting to start our own family.

Like we mentioned before, when that article came out and people were being so mean and negative about a grown-ass, same-sex couple wanting to have our own children, we knew that there was definitely a need for more representation and stories like ours. I began thinking, *If this is how people really feel about gay couples when they are trying to have a baby, I can only imagine what it feels like for folks who don't have support when they want to come out or simply feel seen, heard, and validated.* I can imagine that that kind of feedback would make most people want to go back into their shell.

Building an online community with like-minded people on similar journeys meant that Terrell and I were now committed to living out loud and that we were going to be the representation that we wish we'd had when we were younger. We've always wanted to build up our social media community that we initially cultivated on Facebook because they were the ones who supported us so genuinely and authentically from the beginning. When we chose to expand our content to YouTube, it allowed us to connect with our audience in a more personal and authentic way. With YouTube, we could just be ourselves. We fell into a natural rhythm for ourselves where we would talk about our day-to-day routines, the dynamics of our relationship, and our lives as parents.

We kept at it for two years, and we landed our first brand deal in 2018. Companies had sent us products and things for free before, but we had never set up a deal for compensation. Our very first deal was to partner with an author to promote their children's book for $500. We sat down, talked, and came to the conclusion: "That's one of our car notes—let's do this!" After that first deal, we realized that we had influence, that people were seeking us out for representation and sticking around because of the fun and beauty of our family. Not only could we use our platform to make a difference, but social media could really be a viable means to take care of our family. Slowly but surely, our community grew, and the brand deals started flowing, too.

Our huge tipping point was in December 2018 when we received a call from an executive at Disney World, yes, *the* Disney. They were offering us a deal to shoot a three-day commercial with our family at the theme parks. The only problem was that I was facing a critical moment with my job. There was a company-wide project that required overtime all around, so it was more difficult than usual for me to take leave for the Disney commercial opportunity. On the one hand, I felt like there was unspoken pressure to show up and be reliable for the company. On the other hand, I knew that the future financial security of our family partly relied on my presence.

My choice to bet on our family and fly down to Orlando for the commercial shoot was the nail in the coffin for my job. As soon as I got back, they were all over me trying to get me to put in my notice to quit, but I stuck it out until the episode featuring our appearance on *Wife Swap* debuted in April 2019. That was all the confirmation we needed for me to leave and keep pushing our social media career forward.

We had no idea what was going to come from being on *Wife Swap* as this was our first time on television. But between our episode and the commercial from Disney premiering and also building more buzz, people began flooding our in-box and we could really begin to see how we could create and become a real business. Our commercials were on planes, TV, movie theaters, and we were even on the home page of the official Walt Disney website. By the end of May 2019, our whole summer was filling up with new opportunities.

Eventually, we sought an agent who could help navigate the negotiation process with our brand partners. We needed someone to read the fine print and let us know what we were really getting into while we dealt with every facet of our growing business. We met every agent halfway and showed up prepared. We were never hesitant to ask questions and to challenge things in the negotiation process. We ended up getting signed relatively quickly.

One of our first viral posts was when we shared our wedding story on YouTube. We were completely surprised by how much love we received. We knew from the experience in the *Wall Street Journal* story that viral posts can go to anyone, and they can invite unnecessary negativity.

But then there are times where the right people see it and truly feel what we are sharing. It was beautiful to know that people were being inspired by our marriage and for us to show that two men can create a life and a family together. We were particularly proud that that part of our story went viral because we know that, for so many people, creating a love like ours is not their reality. We heard back from so many people that we inspired them to know that love could be possible for them, too. That kind of feedback pushed us to want to share more of our story because we believe that it is important for people to know that good relationships and faithful partnerships exist.

Some of the greatest love that we have gotten has been from viewers and followers across the continent of Africa. Unfortunately, there are so many countries where same-sex couples are frowned upon. We've heard lots of stories from people who say things like, "I live in a country that doesn't really support who I am, so I often feel alone. Watching your videos gets me inspired and lets me see another avenue for my life."

We had one person who shared that he was in a country where being gay could lead to death. He said, "I watched your video where you all were having spicy conversations with your mothers. Although you guys have been in a world where you felt you had to hide and felt bullied online, to know that you had a safe space with your mothers brought joy to my heart. When I saw the laughs that you guys were sharing with each other, it really made me feel like one day I'm going to be able to create my own family where everyone feels seen and heard." When I saw that comment, I immediately teared up. I could start to see that as the world that I want my children and grandchildren to grow up in.

We've also had feedback from parents who have told us that they're now encouraged to have conversations with their LGBTQIA+ children that they didn't know how to have before watching our social media channels. A huge segment of our audience are also heterosexual couples who share that us just being us inspires them to know that they can have a great family, too.

Even with positive feedback like that, Terrell and I had to learn over time how to put boundaries in place on social media. At first, it was really exciting and things on our pages and channels happened so quickly. I can admit now that I got caught up in going from this regular person who nobody knew to now being known by hundreds of thousands of people.

In the beginning, I would read the comments a lot—probably a little bit too much, to be honest. It was really exciting for somebody who came from a town of less than 4,000 people. But I quickly learned that for every 300 positive comments, there's gonna be that one negative comment that stings. Before I knew it, I'd be arguing with some fool on social media about what they think of me. And I'd start to think, *Maybe we should add more videos about one topic or another or restructure things the way people suggest.*

But then I realized I wasn't paying attention to how I truly felt and I was allowing other people's thoughts and opinions to shape my own. I trained myself not to get too attached to anything that could really wear me down. I don't have any problem taking social media off my phone for a few weeks and just posting the necessary partnerships that we have and immediately logging off when I'm done.

When Terrell and I were going through a tough patch in our relationship and we were sharing that part of our story on our pages, that really solidified what was important to me. We were never inauthentic about what we were going through, but we started to question the need to talk about *everything*. I started to feel like who am I to be sitting up here trying to get validation from social media when I couldn't validate myself?

We started to realize with social media that it can be easy to believe your own hype. The truth is the only difference between us and other people is the number of followers we have and our willingness to be open and transparent about our lives. But that can create a false reality.

We never want people in our audience to be disappointed and to feel like what we are sharing is all a façade. Nor do we want people to feel like they are reaching for perfection when we aren't perfect. So we had to get authentic and deal with the real issues.

After a few years of developing our channels, we became more strategic about how we were sharing our content and we made sure that we weren't sharing anything that we hadn't worked out with each other before posting for our audience. We were still being 100 percent authentic, but we learned through trial and error that we didn't need to go live every time we had something to say. We could take a minute and process what we wanted to share without feeling like we had to be an open book. This also allowed us to be more strategic and intentional with our content and eventually develop specific series or sets of posts around helping our fans get through similar situations.

Eventually, I learned how to get to a point where I use social media as I need to and then I hop off. I now use social media for my own pleasure and enjoyment, and not necessarily for validation. Social media is a vehicle for us to be able to continue to do the work that we set out to do. But I don't have to feed into the negative comments, and I don't have to let them affect me.

Terrell

Social media has earned us a very unique and enhanced lifestyle. We are very blessed to be able to do what we have done. I'm really thankful that it's the source of all the places we've been, the things we've gotten to do, and the special times that we have been able to spend with our kids.

We definitely shared a lot more in the beginning on our social media channels than we do now. We were also a lot younger. But we've honestly had to shift to where we now have three children that we have to be accountable for. We try as best we can to keep our social media visible, and show that our family exists, but we also want to give our kids a sense of privacy. We always want to be respectful and mindful of the things that we're putting out.

There is a sense of pressure to keep cranking out content because we're almost like professional musicians to a certain extent. We've had people tell us, "We follow you because we're living through you and now you're just sharing little bits and pieces. We no longer get the full experience." It's tough because we started off being so open and transparent, but people have to realize that we can't show y'all as much of everything.

We now have to be mindful of how we're doing this because we aren't just reaching thousands anymore.

Our videos reach millions of people and that can be a lot. There are many families who started out the same time we did on social media but they're not here anymore because they got burned out. We definitely don't want to get to that point.

We are always looking for ways of sharing our story and doing things differently. When you don't see us on YouTube as often, we're always working on other things with the goal of getting in front of different audiences. We're trying to branch out with other projects and speaking events. You're holding this book in your hands right now because we want to reach a wider audience to let people know what Black gay love can really look like.

———————

Once we had Ashton and Aria and we decided to include them more in our social media platforms, we were fortunate that most of the people who had been along with us since our first pregnancy were already rooting for us to have children. After they arrived and we were comfortable sharing them with our audience, it was like we had built-in cheerleaders who were happy to come along with us on the ride.

When we started going super viral, it opened

up the doorway for new opportunities and a wider audience—and with that, more opinions that didn't necessarily match ours. When those negative opinions and feedback showed up, we were quick to shut down people who became a little too comfortable talking about our family. We are not above a good clapback, okay? If you go low, you might find we'll be right there on the floor with you. Thankfully, our children are too young to process what's going on, and we do our best to keep them away from any of this kind of negative commentary.

Now that Ashton and Aria are a little older and want to be included in our videos and reels, we lightly prep them: "Most people are happy to enjoy what we are sharing. But there will be some people who are not going to be nice. Even if that happens, we know that we will not let that change the core of who we are."

While we are comfortable sharing our children on social media as a way to inspire people, we have always been intentional about not exploiting or profiting from their exposure. We've always been clear with ourselves and our children that when we share parts of our story on social media, this is simply a way for us to have fun family time. Think of this as a digital baby book.

The good thing that we have learned is that there's not much that we share about the kids other than their birthdays. We don't really talk about the in-depth conversations that we have with them or how we choose to discipline them. We don't divulge that type of information because we have learned to have a good grip on what's appropriate and not appropriate for social media. Sometimes a situation, an experience, a trip, or a bad day doesn't need to be documented. Sometimes we are more than okay with just having memories in our head. Not everything in our lives needs to have a camera recording it for the world.

We don't ever want our children to look back and feel like they had to perform or "be on" when we were having authentic family moments. When they feel like filming something fun with us, we include them, and when they don't, we don't force it. Now being parents for six years, we've had some of the most beautiful, funniest, and most heartwarming conversations with our kids and those private moments never made social media.

Our kids and their future will always be very well taken care of—regardless of how long we choose to be on social media. We are parents first—before anything else. We don't play about them kids! I am very proud to say that I took the lead on creating a family trust and making sure that they were very secure.

Staying Focused on the Big Picture

We've never let social media go to our heads. There has never been a need for us to overdo it. We've always been very clear about what we share on social media and drawing the line with saving and protecting the details of our everyday lives. We certainly are not comparing ourselves to Beyoncé (ha!), but we respect how she shows up as an entertainer, gives incredible shows all over the world, and then she goes back to her private life with no apologies.

Even before we were on social media as public figures, we tended to be more private, especially as it related to our relationship. We have no issue with being super transparent about all the shortcomings that we've had in our relationship and the things that we've had to work through. But we're going to work through them first before the world knows about them because we don't need any extra eyes and ears focusing on our situation. We needed to be focused on what we needed and wanted, instead of listening to the crowd. Having that mentality has kept our conscience clear about the things that we've posted.

We're a very tight-knit family, and we're very selective about the things that we do show people. Our approach to content creation is that we try to show people a different side of what it means to be LGBTQIA+ and parents. It's not really our job to force people to convert or change. Our goal is always to provide insight to people. We want to be an inspiration and to make people feel good about themselves.

The toughest parts of our social media journey have been when, as we invite people into our world, we also have to be prepared to deal with their opinions and assumptions. If we're not careful to keep the two separated, it can really weigh us down—and in truth, at some points it has impacted us. For instance, when we were consistent on YouTube, people were able to see our personality on full display. But in truth, they were only getting a ten-to-fifteen-minute video once a week.

As we were going through very tough times in our marriage and sharing those stories with our audience, people thought that they just knew the intricacies of our relationship, how it worked, and who we were as people. Looking back, we can take some responsibility for not clarifying that this was just a glimpse of the picture. It's very tough to live out loud and to invite so many strangers into your home, and have people start to pick at your insecurities.

The biggest blessing has been having a hand in being able to directly impact the world and being able to shape it in a way that we want for ourselves, our children, and future generations to be able to live in. Everyone wants to be able to impact the world and everyone wants to leave their mark on the world. We all have this uniqueness about us.

Social media has allowed us to share our family in a way that has given us permission and space to heal. There have been a lot of families who have reached out to us and shared their experiences of being broken due to a child or a family member coming out. When we have an opportunity to break down the stereotypes that have been unjustly placed upon the LGBTQIA+ community, in many ways it has allowed for more open conversations that enable families to grow and gain new perspectives. We've been incredibly happy to receive those kinds of emails and messages from people all around the world, thanking us not only for giving a voice to the person who was affected, but also for opening up a new dialogue and vantage point for the family members who weren't open or ready to accept the people in their lives before seeing our story.

We've had moms who have written to us and said, "I have a son who is gay, and for the longest time, I couldn't accept it. I couldn't see it. When I came across you guys, you just made it feel so normal and you weren't aggressive about it. You didn't throw it in my face or try to shove it down my throat. All I could do was respect the beautiful family you guys built. Seeing you two has allowed me to be able to have a different perspective about my own child. And now we're working through this." People tell us that now they're going to therapy and having better conversations in their families. Sharing our lives has been a blessing that has allowed us to be able to bring people together.

Lesson No. 11: You Do You

Jarius

And if I can give y'all a little bit more tea behind the scenes, oftentimes as content creators, we compare ourselves and compete—a lot—with other creators. I know, I know, "Comparison is the thief of joy," but y'all, whether people want to admit it or not, social media is a numbers game. And sometimes it can feel like other creators are judging you and saying things like, "Oh, you don't have a million followers? You can't sit with us." We have learned how to get out of our heads and be practical about how we're letting

social media affect us. You have to figure out how to
do you.

Terrell

Coming from Louisiana, where we like to fight, it's
very different being able to deal with somebody just
on the internet. It's different to be on a platform and
for so many people to look up to you. When somebody says something disrespectful about how we look
or how we show up, there's this expectation that we're
not gonna clap back. People think that just because
we're public figures, we're just gonna be respectful and
not say anything. People might think, *Well, y'all are
putting content out there, so I can feel free to comment.
And I'll be like I got the freedom to comment right back.*

In the beginning, we had other gay couples challenging us and saying, "You're trying to re-create heter-
onormative lifestyles!" We were quick to fire back and
say, "No, we're just trying to discover our own path
to be us and to have kids." These conversations were
wake-up calls for us that we didn't know it all in every
situation. And even with Atlanta being more open,
that didn't necessarily mean that we saw gay couples
walking openly down the street with their families. So

we had to have harder and more truthful conversations with ourselves about "What do we truly want?" and "Can we see creating a family really being a possibility for us here?"

Eventually we were blessed to start finding people with kids and the same kind of family goals who naturally began to gravitate to us. We really wanted to learn and be fulfilled by gaining more knowledge with other people. In time, we felt like we were gaining the tools to be in alignment with people who had similar mindsets and were helping us to continue moving in a positive direction.

One of the biggest things that I've learned from our time on social media is that you have to be able to adapt. Everything in the world changes. By no means does this suggest that we show up inauthentically online. We are still the same raw, vulnerable, and honest couple who people fell in love with. However, we now know how to deal with things in our marriage and our parenting privately.

Sometimes it's tough to stick it out even when what you're doing benefits other people. We could've quit social media a long time ago, but I know that we stick it out because we get those positive messages that come at just the right time and we know that we're inspiring people. It's inspiring when people let us know that seeing one of our videos stops them from doing the unthinkable. We keep doing this because people tell us that before watching our videos, they didn't have hope or they couldn't have relationships with their parents, and now after seeing us living our lives, they know that they can, too.

7

Learning How to
Bet on Ourselves

As much as we love setting an example for other couples and families, we'd be lying if we didn't admit that we feel pressure to be a "perfect" family. And we're guilty of presenting ourselves according to our beliefs around what that ideal is. Our income and livelihood are largely dependent on our reputation and maintaining that becomes even more frightening when the world is judging our every move, outfit, and social media post—and cancel culture is a real thing.

When we first launched ourselves on social media, we naïvely thought that because we were so positive and fun, everyone would like us—and most did! But when we introduced our kids to the world, our audience shifted, and we became more careful about our messaging. We make mistakes, but we largely ignore those who are hellbent on criticizing our kids, our relationship, our faithfulness to God, and pointing out all the wrong things we're doing. It feels like far too many people not only expect us to fail but would find joy in it if we did.

In this chapter, we will talk about how we have learned while building our careers on social media and in all of our business ventures to always bet on ourselves. You have to believe in yourself. Especially with social media, where we've seen people just want to be an instant success. Even though our content may look easy and fun, it has taken a lot of hours, effort, and sometimes tears for us to create the kind of content that we can be proud of.

Between the two of us, Terrell has always been the more ambitious person and always dreams big. Terrell's ambition is one of the things that drew Jarius in, but in the beginning of our relationship, those big audacious dreams scared him at the same time.

Our upbringings have also played a huge role in how we approach our individual dreams and how we began building our lives together. We've worked so hard to be the opposite of our parents in some ways. Obviously, we want to take the best qualities, but in some ways, even the things that we don't like still show up.

Terrell never liked waiting for anything. If his parents said, "Son, you will need to work toward getting a car," he was the kid who had three or four jobs in high school to make that desire happen—*now*. He never liked hearing the word "no"—and still doesn't. His ambition came from wanting things when he wanted them. While as a child, he never wanted for anything, his family didn't have a lot of extra money to spend on vacations or experiences. He wanted to create a new reality for our children and for us to have financial freedom.

In Jarius's family, there was often so much worry and stress about money and being anxious about the future. Being brought up in a household where he was taught to be super cautious in everything, to this day, it's still a struggle for him in our relationship to break out of those fears and worries. In the beginning of our relationship, Jarius was often the one who would say, "Maybe we don't need to push the envelope so much. We've already got these good things going on. We don't need to keep pressing our luck." Having that constant tug-of-war between Terrell's ambition and Jarius's caution made things difficult at first, but eventually Jarius began coming around to seeing and beginning to believe that together there was nothing that we couldn't do.

While we were still in college, we both hit a low point when we both lost our jobs and we had to reach out to our parents for financial help.

Within a few days, Terrell's mom loaned us money to help us with our rent. This was especially hard for us as we tried our best to be independent. But we had no other options. Jarius's mom had already done things for us as well. This was the wake-up call we both needed to become more ambitious and dream bigger because we knew that all we had to lean on was each other.

This setback pushed Terrell even further into declaring, "I'm never going to be in that situation again." As we became adults and eventually parents, that low point in college stuck with both of us and we've always worked incredibly hard to find our way to make things work together. We're very fortunate to say that we've never asked our parents for anything else since that time.

One of the new ventures we took on together was opening up a chain of barbeque restaurants in Georgia. As usual for us, Terrell was five steps ahead of Jarius and thinking far beyond our initial dreams of establishing one location at a time. We discussed the benefits of having a physical business as something that we believed we could have more control over and ultimately it could be something that we could pass down to our children.

At first, Jarius fought the idea of opening up a restaurant. We were already doing so much to keep our social media audience going and engaged. While Jarius was onboard and excited about the idea of building our legacy and our future beyond social media, there were times along this path when he felt caught between two worlds. For him, there were huge questions in his mind, such as, "If I say no to these restaurants, will I stifle Terrell's growth and ambition?" "Am I being fair to myself?" and "Are we doing *too* much?!"

Terrell

Anybody who works with their spouse will tell you it's not going to be rainbows and sunshine. Marriage is hard by itself, so when you add a layer of work and doing something different, naturally you're two different people and you're going to have different perspectives. Naturally, you're going to want to operate on different timelines, just like how we first showed up in our relationship.

For example, if Jarius wakes up and tells me that he

isn't at his best on a specific day, I have to be understanding of that. But then when you have another layer of a business and you have to keep this train moving, even if I'm having a bad day and he has to pick up the slack, it's not always fun to carry the load. But I do it because I know that this is my partner and this is my husband. I know that I have to show up, and I want to lighten the load, but it's not the highlight of my day.

We had to have some hard conversations about how we can be supportive of each other's dreams, exercise some good caution, and still keep our family as our first priority. We are always in a position where we are trying to make sure we manage our health, being a good spouse for each other, having personal time for ourselves, creating couple time with each other, being great parents, and staying on top of our businesses. We often find ourselves asking each other, "We know things are good, so why are we putting so much pressure on ourselves and pulling our lives in so many different directions?" There's always this constant push and pull for us of being glad that we jumped out on faith to take on another great partnership or opportunity and also being completely exhausted on the other side and being real with ourselves and asking, "Did we really need to do that, too?!"

Even with choosing to open our restaurants after the

pandemic, we've always believed that if you put your best foot forward, things are going to work out. We knew the risks and we were willing to take a chance on ourselves—yet again. We truly believe that when you do things with pure intent and in alignment with God, he always makes a way. Crazy enough, there hasn't been much that we've tried to do that has not turned out well.

So many people dream of creating a business or a side hustle with their partner, but we gon' tell y'all the truth: This ain't for the faint of heart. Our work together is an up-and-down process every single day. There are some days we work extremely well together, and then there are other days where we can't stand each other. We're grateful that there are more good days than bad, but each day gives us a new challenge and we have learned to be up for whatever the day gives us.

Jarius

If you're going to work with your spouse, you have to be truthful about your dynamic. A lot of times in relationships, we jump into things just from an emotional perspective. We do things with our heart, not necessarily our mind. It's easy to think, *I've been with this person for X amount of time, so we can go into business together*. But if you go into business with your spouse without thinking through all those dynamics, you can ignore a lot of things that you wouldn't ignore if you were looking for a business partner.

If I were looking to go into business with you, we'd have a whole interview process. We'd make sure we blend together and that our visions are cohesive, but I don't think we do that when we look at our spouse. We just assume that love is going to be enough to get us through.

If someone was looking to us for business advice, number one, just be truthful about whether you and your relationship can really sustain the level of complexity that's going to come along with trying to work with someone that you also sleep with. I'm sure that Terrell gives me a lot of passes on things because, at the end of the day, we still have to go home to each other. We know that we are both willing to put up with more things that we wouldn't put up with from someone who we were not in love with.

When we first decided to leave our nine-to-five jobs, we worked together quite well because we were passionate, and it was exciting and new to discover how we were going to build this platform together. When we decided to go full-time with social media, it felt freeing for us to not have to answer to anyone and to be home with our children. We reached this incredible goal of creating and settling into our lives on our own terms. We saw the money that we were making and realized that it was so much more fun to create something that we never could have done in our corporate careers. We saw the pieces of the puzzle coming together, and it was exciting. As we continued to grow and settle into our groove, we learned how to balance our priorities.

But even with that balance, it still takes some effort for us to park our work at the front door. That separation between work and home gets hard because someone is always emailing or texting us at all times of the day. Our management company and most of the brands that we work with are on the West Coast. With their workdays three hours behind us, it can be quite a challenge to shut things off and not let our schedule become so overwhelming.

Lesson No. 12: Learning How to Bet on Ourselves

Nobody sets out to have a dream of creating their own social media content or business and watch it fail. We know from our own stops and starts with several business ventures that everybody is doing the best they can. Having that mindset has allowed us to be more gracious with our partners, our employees, and everyone around us who is helping us to make our dreams come true. We both agreed that we would not be in the business of working ourselves to death. Terrell's dad was the ultimate example of being part of that generation who worked, worked, and then worked some more. We know that we are not alone with families who worked hard, but in truth, with working long hours, it's only a matter of time before you have to sacrifice the things that matter most, like spending time with your family. Nothing is worth it if you are running yourself into the ground and you're not good enough to show up for the things that are most important to you.

We are firm believers that you really have to understand your why and know how to set up good boundaries for yourself and your dreams. We know that our goals are focused on creating generational wealth for our children and prioritizing their happiness and well-being. That's why we prioritize time for vacations and their extracurricular activities, and we make sure that we're not sacrificing their core memories.

We have learned to have such an appreciation for people who can say that they have started from the ground up. Everyone wants to talk about building an empire, but they do not have a true understanding of what it actually takes to build original content;

form great relationships with investors, managers, and employees; and sustain your success over time. So we have learned to appreciate our glow-up and to always continue learning and growing from others around us who are doing it well.

8

Nobody Wins When the Family Feuds

We'll be honest: Some days, we flat out don't like each other. There, we said it. Hear us out, though. When nearly every part of your life is intertwined with your partner's, it's natural to want some space every now and then—even if you can't imagine going to sleep each night without them. But even when our marriage is hard, we keep forging ahead with an eye on the good parts. We remind ourselves that the positive far outweighs the bad—and that's what's most important. In some capacity or another, we work on our marriage every day so that when conflicts arise, we've poured enough happiness into our cup that we can tap into that reserve.

When you pour into yourself, you'll have more to share and give to your partner when they're feeling down or itching to start a spat. We discovered that bringing our families together was no different than planning a party and combining friends. For us, it was almost like asking, "Where's everybody going to sit?" "How are we all going to mingle?" and "How's it going to go?"

Our families met for the first time during Christmas in 2013. Terrell's core family includes his father, his mother, and his sister, and Jarius's inner-circle family members are his mother and his grandmother. We also have close first cousins in both families who we've come to enjoy spending time with.

Once our children came into the picture, we had to make sure that people were showing up to our village in a way that was respectful and made sense for us. We knew that the kids would be something that could unite us or completely tear us apart. Because we both knew that if there was ever an issue concerning our kids or our parenting, we'd be ready for war! Obviously in both of our families we feared there would be a lot of opinions and differences as they relate to us being together. But at the end of the day, the kids are innocent. We had high hopes for the family coming together and supporting us, but we quickly found out that those high hopes needed to turn into high boundaries. We've always been clear that we will never allow anyone to make us or our children feel belittled, demeaned, or less than. At times, those kinds of bad behaviors put us in a position of needing to put up those walls and sometimes even cutting folks off.

In particular for our parents, we know that it was tough for them at times to allow us to grow up and become men. It has been quite the struggle for them to see us beyond the little boys who they used to take care of and allow us to be husbands and fathers. The line drawn between childhood and adulthood with our parents has often been quite blurry. Without fail, one of our parents will test us and try to assert that they are still in charge and that they know best. And we respectfully shut the test down every time.

In this chapter, we'll discuss how we've learned to create realistic expectations around our families, establish boundaries, and make peace with who we are in relation to our families now.

Terrell

One of the biggest lessons that we've learned with our family is that you have to meet people where they are.

Jarius and I realize that our parents were raised in a very different time. Our parents often believe that as their children, we are indebted to them. My mother is famous for saying things like, "I gave birth to you, so you owe me the world," or "You've only got one mother!" And I've often turned that right around and replied, "Well, you've only got one son." But in all honesty, these are generational beliefs that they were also taught growing up. So it becomes a chain reaction. My mom and I have had a lot of back-and-forth discussions about what it means for us to have a relationship and manage expectations now that I am an adult. The truth is that, as we grow and change, so does our relationship with our parents, whether they want it to or not. My role is to be a great dad, be a great spouse, and live my best life. I hope that my children express gratitude not by trying to "give me the world" (I mean, what a huge ask!), but by existing in the world in a way that is authentic to them and a benefit to their communities.

Unfortunately our families have also heavily scrutinized Jarius and me because of where life has taken us. People in our families have accused us of acting funny or saying that we've changed—this is classic for many people in the Black community that we realized once we discussed this with trusted friends. When you get a new title at work, buy a new home, or become successful beyond other people's expectations, the gloves start coming off and the sneak disses enter the chat.

You would hope that family would want to see you do well and be successful, but we've had family members whisper behind our backs and say things like, "Why are y'all trying to be so different?" Our response has typically been, "Nobody's ever gotten anywhere by staying in the same spot! Why is it not okay for us to want better for ourselves and to make choices that benefit us and our children?" Isn't that everyone's goal? So we've become more unapologetic about how we move because we do want better for ourselves and our children. Sometimes this means putting up a hard boundary and cutting off communication with some folks, prepping our kids a bit before interacting with some of our family members, and when we need to, we got a few clapbacks in our back pocket that are ready when folks act out of line.

We know that our families love us and want the best for us; however, I do realize as a parent it is difficult not to see your child as the little baby who used to need you for everything and to truly respect them and their opinions once they reach adulthood. So often for parents, they believe that a mark of their success is that their children still need and depend on them. We have been fortunate enough not to have to heavily depend on my parents since 2013. So it's created this weird dynamic of how our family members view us and are able to show up for us—and I'm sure many of you guys can relate to that.

It's also difficult at times to hear when family members make homophobic comments and people laugh and intentionally or unintentionally make us uncomfortable. We've also had to get bold with a few relatives who smiled in our faces but would make their religious beliefs and prejudices about us known to others.

Even with all of our success and building our family, we've had to put some hard lines in the sand. As we have become more confident with who we are, we certainly were not going to let anyone—least of all our family members—take us backward and make us feel less than with their limiting beliefs and ideologies.

Oftentimes it feels like we lose a bit of the human side in people's eyes and are looked at as "Terrell and Jarius" versus who we are individually. Sometimes we wonder: If we still had our traditional sales jobs and social media was not a thing, would our family members treat us differently? Right now, there has not been anyone who has achieved the amount of success that we have, especially at such a young age, and to be honest, that creates a lot of animosity.

We've had some family members who have joked, "What do you give the person who has everything?" We've never asked for designer things or much at all for that matter. In fact, Jarius is notorious for simply asking for underwear and socks. We just want quality time with our families. I know we don't want for money, but we still want to feel loved, and supported. It's frustrating and sad at times because I think sometimes it gets lost on them that Jarius and I are still normal human beings.

Enforcing the Grandparent Rules

Now that both of our mothers are more active in helping us with the kids, we've also learned to put boundaries in place when they interject their opinions about how we are raising and disciplining our children. Sometimes they have given feedback about what we choose as their consequences for their actions. They have asked things such as, "Do you really need to take their toys away?" or "Did you really have to make a big deal about that?" Particularly with Jarius's mom, being here live and in person with us now in Atlanta definitely gives her a different perspective on how we operate on a daily basis. We've had to establish clear rules with them about our expectations for them as grandparents. We are more than happy to welcome them into the village, but we want them to have full trust in us that we know what is best for our children and how we want to see them show up in the world.

We've also been careful not to put our children in the crossroads of any breakdowns that we have with our parents. We try to resolve things the best way that we can. Even though people in our families have a tendency to drag issues out for years before resolving them, we make sure that we do our part to right any wrongs that we are responsible for and do our best to move forward peacefully.

Terrell

While we have achieved financial success, I still need emotional support from my parents. Even as a grown man with my own husband and children, there are some days when I just need my mom. I want to be able to call my mom and speak with her like a peer, with real-world adult-size problems, and maybe troubleshoot a few of hers, too. After all, she's now at a point in life where she wants to be more independent.

My mother was the first person who I came out to, and I was honored that she kept that secret until I was ready to share it with the world. Now that I am a father and want her to be more connected with our children, I'm looking for new ways to bridge the gap between us as we both move toward our best lives.

Another relationship—my relationship with my father—often makes me think about how I am raising my own children and wonder how they're going to feel about me and Jarius when they grow up. Oftentimes I empathize with my father because he lost his own father when he was very young. He was raised by a mother who was a no-nonsense type and very direct, so it makes sense that he raised me in a way that I felt was too rigid.

Two years ago, he also experienced a life-changing event that nearly cost him his life. He was involved in a boating accident in which he was stranded in the water for hours, hanging on to a post for dear life. He lost his best friend that day, and his life changed completely. I tried to be there for him as much as I could. I thought that going through that tragic loss and traumatic experience would help him to view life differently and better appreciate moments knowing tomorrow isn't promised.

But unfortunately, we've continued to fall back into the repetitive and toxic cycle of our relationship. I know that my father loves me, but I don't think he knows *how* to love me or how to show his version of affection. I pray it's something that works itself out on its own with time. I want him to be proud of the man I have become as well as the father I am. While things are not perfect, most kids I knew growing up did not have their father, so I will forever appreciate him for being there my entire life.

My sister is five years younger and is the complete opposite of me. From my college admission to the present day of taking care of my family, I've done everything all by myself. Meanwhile, my sister is often dependent upon my parents. It has made me often wonder if my sexuality were different, would my parents be as open to supporting me as they have my sister?

Jarius

We just want to pour into the people who pour into us. We don't want to force things. We now know that our family members do not have an unlimited pass to say, think, or just do whatever they want. But with family, sometimes you have to meet people where they are.

For example, I willingly choose to take care of my grandmother and make sure that she is good. Although I had to take a step back from our relationship a couple of years ago, I still do not want to see her struggle. So when she lost her significant other to dementia shortly after I stopped communicating with her, she was left with no way to pay for her car, which he had just purchased for her. She was also in need of some significant repairs to her home, and Terrell and I had to step in to save the day or she was going to be car-less and with water leaking into her home.

While we were happy to help, she literally just acknowledged within the last year that Terrell and I are a married couple. I've made my peace with the fact that it is an extremely tough task to change the mindset of a woman who is over seventy years old, but it doesn't mean it doesn't hurt. As long as I don't feel disrespected, I've learned to meet her where she is and deal with the parts of her I feel like dealing with. My grandmother is one of the funniest people on the planet to me, and no one brings me the amount of joy that she does when she gets going. But I also understand that there's another side of her that if I call her at the wrong time of the day, she is still gonna yell at me like I'm a child.

It can be hard to hear that it's necessary to put up boundaries and sometimes to even end communication with toxic family members. At some point you have to realize that you have to put yourself first. I strongly believe that prioritizing my mental health when it comes to my family puts me in the best place to receive these unexpected wins, big and small.

When you are paving a new path, it's natural to want everybody in your family to come along with you. But because we are committed to growing and evolving beyond what we've known, it's often hard for people in our families to comprehend that. If you are going to be brave enough to forge a new path, you also have to be brave enough to go down that path by yourself. You have to be willing to understand that not everybody is brave enough to follow behind you, or they may have challenges on their own path that they need to conquer before your paths can converge again. Although this felt hard for us in the beginning, for our family members who did respect what we were doing, there were some beautiful relationships that we were able to form with new clarity, joy, and understanding.

Lesson No. 13: No Apologies Necessary

We pour everything that we have into our families. But there is a point where that kind of blind loyalty and devotion can become toxic and affect everything around you. Even if someone has a certain title in your family, they still have to show up and respect you.

Being successful also makes it hard to be able to see a person's true intent. We're the first ones to break that kind of traditional mold of moving beyond a nine-to-five job or pursuing a corporate career.

Even now, we continue to keep our close circle very small. The biggest thing that people forget is that we're human, and we still have fears about how people will receive and accept us in the world.

We have also learned that we do not have to be apologetic for just existing. We do our best to show up in the world and be open, loving, and kind to our family members and everyone around us. But we are no longer interested in pleasing everybody and making everyone feel comfortable with our lives. We've got a family to raise and dreams to build—and we aren't going to change our dreams to fit anyone else's expectations.

With our families, we've also learned that it is more than okay to say no—even with our parents. Family is what you make of it, and you also get to choose family that does not consist of your blood relatives to give you the support that you need. So often people try to fit a circle into a triangle and make excuses for bad behavior from their families. It is more than okay for you to discover and celebrate what the healthiest form of family is for you.

9

You Gotta Give Each Other Space to Grow

Have you ever heard of the "seven-year itch"? It's a phenomenon where, after seven blissful years of marriage, a duo's happiness can drop off, and they're no longer on the same page. We always thought it was a cliché, but we're here to tell you that the itch is real—and affected us, big-time. We're not the same people we were when we were bright-eyed eighteen-year-olds. Our thoughts and beliefs have shifted, and we each have new convictions. Ultimately, we realized that an evolving mindset is helpful to forge a lasting relationship.

Getting through the "seven-year itch" required two and a half years of therapy and a lot of emotional processing to relearn who we each are, together and as individuals. In this chapter, we will explore how we had to learn the difference between compromise and sacrifice, and how we learned what to do when "compromise" simply feels like one person is winning and the other is losing.

———————

During the seventh year of our relationship, Ashton and Aria had just turned one, and we were struggling a lot. There were so many moving pieces happening for us at the time. We were just getting started on social media, and we were now being grouped together a lot. We were no longer individuals. Our Instagram name was literally who we were becoming.

Shortly after we wrapped *Wife Swap*, we were approached to do our own TV pilot. We were also fairly new to Atlanta still, and getting pulled in a million exciting, but different, directions. The two of us were trying to find ourselves. Our viewpoints were changing, our communication was slacking, and a lot of tension was building up as we were trying to understand each other while we were also growing.

We found it hard to find friends who shared the same kinds of responsibilities that we did, since few of them had kids and many were still in their out-until-two-or-three-o'clock-in-the-morning era. They could wake up whenever, and to us, it looked like they had the freedom to just be individuals.

Terrell

After Ashton and Aria were born, I was struggling a lot with my individuality. I love my kids to death and I love being in a relationship. But there was still a part of me that wanted to know what it felt like to be free and not worry if my husband was going to feel some sort of way if I decided to hang out one night. But I knew I couldn't be that irresponsible. Remember that we got together just weeks after we got to college, so I never really had the opportunity to find myself or explore my independence.

My parents argued a lot when I was growing up. So when I got into my relationship with Jarius, my mentality was let me do what I can do to make sure that we are on the same page. I often pushed my own viewpoints to the side for the sake of peace. Or if I would challenge back, ultimately I would just give in. We were still learning how to navigate through our complexities as two men with different religious perspectives, family backgrounds, and expectations. So it was still challenging to figure out a happy medium for our relationship.

Jarius is very traditional, and he would always say, "Terrell, here are my guardrails!" I would be quick to challenge his viewpoints, which I felt were based on old opinions and environments that we'd outgrown. In the middle of our arguments, Jarius would often present his opinions on what a relationship should look like as facts, and I would literally have to combat that by going to my trusted friend Google to bring up divorce rates and statistics about his "facts."

I'll admit that during that time I began to rebel in our relationship. I started feeling like I was losing myself. Once I came out and was able to live more freely, I wanted to make up for everything that I'd missed. My desire to do new things and make my circle of friends larger began creating a huge struggle between us. I thought I knew who I was at the time, but ultimately I didn't. I wanted to do what I wanted to do when I wanted to do it. I started to ask myself questions like, "What is marriage?" "Is this how I'm going to spend the rest of my life?" and "Am I always going to feel like I'm being restricted?"

Jarius

You never really know who you're dating or married to until you get close to the seven-year mark. At that point any façade left over from past phases of life fades and the real person starts to come to the surface.

I grew up by myself, so I was always good with solitude. But I always longed for love and companionship. Once I found Terrell when we were in college, he was all I needed. Terrell grew up with a huge friend group and he's also very social. I knew that he craved having a full friend circle, and I never wanted to deny him that. But I grew up with secrecy all around me. From my mother's relationships to my own. So I knew with him loving and choosing to be in a relationship with me, he had to adapt to me being more introverted.

During this time in our relationship, Terrell got really close with a friend who I did not like. I was fine with the overall friend group, but when they became close, there started to be more consideration for that friend than there would be for me at times. This particular person became the common denominator for a lot of challenges that we were having in our relationship.

Y'all, I was resentful as fuck. So when Terrell started talking about how restricted he felt and wanting to spend more time with his friends, my thought process was, "You wanted all of this, too!" We were working really hard to make our relationship work and now Terrell wanted to branch off from it!? This was one of the first times we really had a friend group and it would make me frustrated when he and this one friend started separating from the group. Call it being jealous, but something didn't sit right with me about it.

I was especially thrown off since Terrell never wanted me to have my own friends because he felt as if everyone ended up liking me. So it felt so unfair to me when he then wanted to toss that thought pattern out the window now that he had this dude. I expected Terrell to be more considerate of my feelings and to make sure that I was clear about where I stood in our relationship, but he wasn't really doing that at the time.

Terrell

It was somewhat easier for me to connect with our friend group at that time in our relationship. And this particular friend group came along right as I was feeling more and more closed off from the world. I needed the time to share hobbies, activities, and of course, the latest gossip with people who I could part from at the end of the day. Eventually, one person in the group became my best friend who I could talk with about how I was changing and evolving. Before this point, when we had issues or tension, Jarius and I did our best to go directly to each other. But when our viewpoints started to change, it was hard to talk about how I was feeling directly with him.

I believed that it was unrealistic to think that your partner could be your best friend. Everyone needs to be able to relate to someone they are not romantically connected to. Jarius was not happy about this. And I was not understanding of his feelings. I kept thinking, *Why is it so hard for you to find your own person you can talk with?*

Jarius

I've never felt more depressed in my entire life than I did during that time. I felt like our house wasn't a safe space anymore. Every day, I was waiting for an argument. Terrell started asking questions like, "What does a married couple *really* look like?" or "Do you have to be committed to this one person forever?" He was going through a phase where he was questioning everything that he'd ever been taught. And I didn't sign up for all that.

I knew that we couldn't move forward until we figured out that situation with the friend because I felt so strongly about it. I remember telling Terrell, "Either you're gonna get rid of this person or you're going to lose your family. So you need to figure it out!"

Terrell

I was unrecognizable to Jarius at the time. I knew that if I was hanging out with someone outside of our relationship, his mind was going to wander, no matter who it was. Honestly, my best friend at the time didn't help. I felt like I was going to lose Jarius and my family over this friendship. So I had to really dig deep and figure out if this friendship was worth it. It ultimately became a full-circle moment when I was wrestling with how much I wanted to experience more freedom in my life, but I also knew that I wanted to father my kids and stay loyal to my husband.

I had to ask myself three honest questions: *Is it too late? Is it all worth it?* and *Do I really want to shatter everything I've built?*

Ultimately, I knew that I wanted to put my best foot forward for my marriage. I was very resentful about having to end a friendship that meant a lot to me. But there wasn't a way for me to maintain that friendship without sacrificing my family. It was really a no-win situation. I had to scale back and realize that my family was worth so much more than just a momentary high.

Jarius

Our kids definitely became the light switch for us to keep figuring things out. Even after Terrell ended the friendship, we knew we didn't want to keep bringing trauma to ourselves or our children. So we had to keep coming back to our foundation and asking ourselves, "What is important for our relationship and how are we going to keep being these amazing fathers that we want to be?"

Now we are learning to manage the inevitability of challenges and breakdowns in our relationship. Back when we were young hotheads and we were fresh in our relationship, we used to squabble about everything. When we were new parents and low on sleep, everything deserved a response. We knew each other's trigger points, and we didn't care about hitting them. But now we know when it's too far. We don't have to hurt each other. We can get our point across in a way that's not disrespectful and we don't have to tear each other down. We ask ourselves now, "Is this really a big deal?"

Another thing that has really helped us is that our current friend group has the same goals and values as us. We definitely don't need everybody to think the same way that we do. But we want to be around others on a similar path. Most of our current friends have their own businesses and have ambitions. More importantly, they fully support our union, so we can trust that they'll honor and respect our feelings. I definitely don't feel pressured or threatened the way that I used to.

Creating Our Chosen Family

Creating a chosen family didn't exactly come naturally to us. We had to first learn how to trust people, since we have always been so private and self-reliant. We always thought our problems were our problems, and while we're open and honest online, we share less with others in person. Jarius had the most hesitations about trusting and confiding in others, but we've finally found our people and built a community from there.

Jarius

It's really tough sometimes when you're unable to figure out the true intent of every single person that's around you. We've had to learn the hard way that the quality and the expectations that we have in our friendships *have* to be a lot different now. As we've grown, we know that we had a lot of friendships in the past that we put too much into. We have realized that we both dive into things because we don't feel that we have a strong family unit. Our friends often became our family, and at times they were the only people we had.

Over time we said to each other, "In our next relationship, we should not do that because it didn't turn out well for these reasons." Now we're more selective when it comes to who we allow in our space, and we've become even more so because of our children.

Terrell

I do think that we can have successful friendships and relationships with other parents. They don't have to be gay or lesbian either. But shared experiences mean a lot nowadays, and I hate to say this, it almost makes you want to be friends with people who understand where you are because they are in it, too.

Sometimes it's easier when you have friends in the industry—especially if you take competition out of the equation—because it helps you to understand and to be able to better relate with people. Then there is no expectation of anything. It's harder to be friends with people outside the industry, in my opinion. There are times where it works beautifully and where things just make sense, but it's also difficult when you have a very nontraditional life.

As you get older, just like with dating, it's harder to make friends. Do you make friends on the internet? Do you date somebody on the internet? Where do you go to find like-minded people?

I used to beat myself up about it because I thought that I should be able to have all these different relationships. I quickly realized that that was probably what I desired in my teens and early twenties, thinking that you should have a group of people you can go out with and you should able to party with and all this stuff. As I settle into my real adult age I now know that I would much rather have one person who truly knows me, who truly knows my children, who I can truly depend and lean on, than being surrounded by a whole bunch of people who I just have surface friendships with.

Jarius

The number of friends that you have when you're in college and high school is so different from the number of friends that you have when you are in your thirties and forties. There are times when I miss being free enough to just pull a group of people together and say, "You know what? Tonight I feel like turning on Cardi B and twerking for my life." We can still do that, but as parents, we have to plan for those kinds of carefree experiences.

These days nine o'clock be rolling around and I'm ready to go to bed. As long as I'm doing things with pure intent, I'm okay with whatever God is moving around me, and whether he's taking something or adding something to it, I'm okay with just being in the process.

There's a country thing that my family used to say a lot: "You keep on living and you keep on experiencing life and you'll see how things shape out." I've seen having a whole bunch of people around me and I've seen having not a lot of people around me, and I've seen how it comes and goes. So there's no need for me to stress out about it now. When God's ready for me to have more solid people around me, I am open to it. I'm not forcing anything any longer.

Lesson No. 14: You Gotta Give Each Other Space to Grow

Every married couple has their problems from time to time. We had to learn how to balance each other's energy, wants, and needs. Most of all, we've learned to respect each other as partners. Trust us, we know how easy it is to get caught up in parenting, social media, work, and social lives. Before you know it, you've missed out on huge things that are important to each person—and have done damage in the process.

We met each other at age eighteen, and now we're in our early thirties. We are much different people than who we were as college freshmen. If you are not willing to acknowledge and recognize that your partner is going to change over time, you may look up one day and not recognize them at all.

We've had to learn over time how to move as a unit. We eventually knew what we wanted—a loving marriage, kids, a good living, a stable life for our children, a happy home. Creating time in your relationship to talk about your previous relationships, the relationship models that you grew up with (or not!), and your expectations are important things during those early stages in your relationship. Knowing those critical aspects of a person will help you understand where they're coming from later down the line and point you toward possible solutions. (Or it may save you from being that person who is posting on social media about somebody wasting their time!) We want you to be in a relationship that can go the distance and will help you to grow and evolve.

Conclusion

Protecting Our Family—and Living Out Loud

Fifty years ago, it would have been impossible for us to become legal parents of our children as a same-sex couple. We can't even begin to say how thankful we are to the pioneers in the LGBTQIA+ community who fought bravely against antiquated laws and made our dream of becoming a family possible.

But even with all the progress, there's still so much work to be done. With all of the anti-gay and anti-trans laws that are currently up for legislative debate, we know we can't sit back and get comfortable—especially if we want our children to grow up happy, healthy, and well adjusted. There are still so many unfair practices around adoption, surrogacy, and fostering children that most straight, cisgender folks don't even have to think about, but these practices work to keep our queer community in the shadows.

In this chapter, we are going to share our journey continuing the fight for everyone's right to create and become a family. We'll share the lessons that we learned around understanding that families are different—and how we celebrate those differences every day, how we remain proud of who we are as an LGBTQIA+ family, and how we welcome other people to see the joys and the struggles in our experience.

———

We don't subscribe to stereotypical gender roles within our family, and we don't fit neatly into anyone's boxes. We're both masculine men and natural-born leaders. At the start of our marriage, we admittedly almost killed each other over who was in charge before we figured out how to work together to run a household—but honestly, that's no different than any other couple who fusses over household duties on a regular basis.

Our biggest identity challenge is the fact that we're part of not one, but two historically marginalized sub-communities as we are both Black and gay. Because so many people value their identities (and rightfully so), it's how we see ourselves. I mean, how often have you tried to conceal a certain facial feature until someone offhandedly points it out! With central characteristics such as race and sexuality, it's likely that people will enter the conversation ready to put you in a box. Suddenly, being gay overshadows everything we go through as Black people. Yet the "gay agenda" doesn't give us protection from being unnecessarily pulled over by the police. At the same time, we struggle to feel comfortable in traditional gay spaces that don't acknowledge Black people's incredible impact on the culture.

We're proud of who we are as a couple and a family, and with our relationship with God. We deserve to be recognized for what brings us together versus what separates us. It's our job to walk in our purpose and show what that looks like. The world will catch up.

Terrell

There are times when we have to ask ourselves, "Is what we're doing making a huge difference?" "Is it appreciated?" and "Is it worth it?" We're still navigating how to create this beautiful life that we want for ourselves and our kids. But we know it's not beautiful to everyone. Everything we do is often ripped apart. From people asking why two Black men would want to be together to particularly audacious people asking why we used white surrogates and why our kids have lighter skin than us. Those negative comments can chip away our confidence—and those chips online can spill over into real life.

Every time our kids start a new school year, there's always a little bit of fear that we have as parents. You never know someone's true intentions or their beliefs. Whenever you're putting your kids in a new environment, even if it's just a few doors down from kindergarten to first grade, we have to be okay with who we're leaving our kids with. It can be incredibly scary to think that our precious babies could be bullied or underserved at school, where we can't hit back and aren't able to shield them.

We've always been very protective of our children, both on and off social media, because people can have bias against us with no way for us to know it. It's hard to balance what we share at times and not worry about whether the wider audience is comfortable. When there was more criticism and focus on the kids, we had to reevaluate how and why we were sharing them with our audience in the first place. Similar to how we wouldn't bring our kids with us if we were meeting someone in person for the first time, we feel the same way with social media. With everything that's going on in the world, we're just trying to do the best we can to gain some sort of reassurance that our kids aren't going to be isolated or made to feel different. So much of how we are received in the world depends upon the world's perception of our lives and our livelihood. And it's no longer just me and Jarius. We have three kids that we need to figure out how to navigate through life with.

It's never been a secret for Aria and Ashton that they have two dads. But it's not like we sit our kids down and then have big, difficult conversations about what it does and does not mean to be gay. Instead, we fortify our children with confidence by having *honest* conversations with them at a level that they can understand (and when Aspen is old enough, we'll do the same with her, too).

One summer, on a family trip to Disney World, we had an opportunity to meet one of the Disney princesses. As Aria was talking with her, the woman innocently said, "I see you have your guardsmen with you," as a part of her character. Aria wasted no time and responded, "No, that's my dad, my daddy, and my big brother. I have two dads!" This was not anything that we specifically taught her to say, so it was a proud moment for me and Jarius to see how she stood up for our family, quickly, clearly, and kindly. The princess smiled at all of us and gave her a hug.

Once you have kids, you learn that they're picking up conversations. Jarius and I used to think that we were talking in code when we were in the front seat of the car. We quickly found out just how much they understood when we heard them repeating parts of our conversation later on. So we do our best to model kindness toward each other, our kids, and other people. We don't approach teaching things to our children in a state of panic. We don't respond to them in an uproar. We're also teaching them the basics of respect and understanding that everyone in this world looks different and it's perfectly okay. We take the time to talk with our children about how not to make an outburst and to know the appropriate time to ask a question or make a request. Just like any other parent, we answer them as honestly as possible, and we teach them how to be good human beings.

When it comes to being affectionate in public and explicitly showing that we are a same-sex couple, I'll be honest, y'all. It's still somewhat challenging for me at times. At the beginning of our relationship, it was a point of contention for Jarius and me. He used to say, "If I was a girl, you wouldn't be embarrassed to hold my hand." But in all honesty, I probably wouldn't engage in too much PDA either way. I've never been that person who is outwardly affectionate. I love spending time with friends, but I'm more of a dap-you-up kind of guy than the one to give you a big hug hello. It hurt that my partner wasn't feeling loved, but there's also always a fear in the back of my head that if we are in a restaurant and someone clocks me as gay, they may do something to hurt us. It sucks to live in a world where you have to operate from fear.

When I talked to Jarius about it, he was understanding. Any hate we've faced, we've faced together. So I'm not afraid to say it didn't come naturally for me to want to kiss my husband in public in fear that someone would want to hurt us. I know that some people will chew me out for not "living authentically." Some people ask, "Are you really an activist?" or "How are you really trying to change the narrative when you can't live in the truth of who you are?" These are some of the same questions that I've asked myself and I'm now able to move beyond acting from a place of fear. I understand the importance of sharing my love in public for society as a whole—and how it moves the needle forward.

However, I cannot be naïve about the fact that there's a whole world of people out there who genuinely want to cause harm. The faster the world catches up, the better we will all be as a human race. But honestly, I still think we have a ways to go. We want to make sure that we get home to our kids safely. That's always our top priority.

Jarius

Some of our family members have asked over the years, "Why didn't you feel comfortable telling me that you are gay?" We've had to challenge those same people back and ask, "In what spaces did you make it comfortable for either one of us to do that?" The room often gets real quiet after that comeback. We've had to have those hard conversations and let people know that it takes an incredible amount of courage to stand up and be who we are. Even with family, we still have to determine who gives us a true safe space to stand in and live fully in our truth.

There are a multitude of things that you have to consider when you're doing your work in public. I also feel that in order to be the change you want, you have to lead the charge. But then you also have to look back on the history of people who have led the charge and some of these people have lost their lives in the process. So we have to choose wisely. We have to think about how we can promote change on and off social media and still authentically live our lives.

We are no strangers to what it means to have to

deal with injustices because of our race, culture, and appearance, and how to band together, too. More often than not, in the Black community, when you see something that affects another Black man or woman, I know for sure that another brother or sister will show up to help figure out a solution.

But when issues specifically impact the Black gay community, the tone shifts to, "Well, that ain't got nothing to do with me and that's not my fight." It doesn't feel fair because we're always standing up for the rights of *all* Black people. When we hear about people being murdered or attacked at concerts or gay clubs, we're disappointed that there's not the same kind of uproar from members of our community. Nobody is ready to tear down the world for that Black person. It almost feels like we're just left to fend for ourselves.

Terrell

Being a good ally is about asking yourself, "How would I want to be treated?" or "How would I want to be able to maneuver in life?" It's really just the same things that you would do to support your friend, bearing anything that they're going through, finding out how that can translate, and finding out what the specific person needs and how they specifically need to be supported.

It's understanding that life is scary for everyone right now, and we're all essentially going through the same thing. You don't have to be part of a specific community to empathize and understand what someone could be going through or put yourself in those shoes. When *Roe v. Wade* was struck down, we were pissed. We're not women, but we don't have to be in the situation to understand when something isn't right. For someone to be supportive is just understanding that it's not equal.

Not every kind of support has to be a donation or a protest. It could simply be if you see someone in the community across your social media timeline, you can leave a heart or a kind comment.

Simply put, as long as you understand it's not equal and that there's a problem, then I think that you've already taken the first step toward becoming an ally by just knowing that there's an issue.

Jarius

Even though I'm a part of the LGBTQIA+ community, I understand and now have awareness that trans people have a much different fight than I do. And I don't understand every facet of it. I don't understand what their shoes are like to walk in. But at the same time, I can understand, too, that if something happens that is not right, who am I to just sit back and not say anything, especially when I have the ability to be able to touch a lot of people?

I do think that we all have a responsibility to be cognizant and aware of how, even though something may not be specific to you, it affects other people, and you can't just sit back and do nothing until it affects somebody in your family.

But it's not enough just to understand that it's a problem. We know it's a problem, and you know it's a problem, but then what are you doing to consciously help to make it not a problem? If you know that there are problems, go out and vote to improve the circumstances, because a lot of it starts with the laws that are specifically in your state. It's just understanding that there are not people in power who protect us, but we have the power to change that by the people we vote for. So be conscious about that, but then also if you're seeing injustices happen within the community, call them out.

Don't just sit there and just be like, "Well, I know it's wrong and I know that shouldn't be happening, but I'm not going to get in it because I ain't got nothing to do with that." We have to actually do stuff to stop it.

Lesson No. 15: Don't Just Stand By— You Can Do Something Today!

Too often people think that the only way to support the LGBTQIA+ community is by attending pride parades or being more vocal during pride month. But the greatest support that we can have is for people to simply have an open mind. We are still living in very scary times where everyone's rights, from women's reproductive rights to affirmative action, are being threatened and challenged every day.

But when you ignore the human element of an issue just because you're not part of a specific community, it's easy to forget we are all essentially moving through the same fears and frustrations. You don't have to understand every little detail about what it means to live life as a member of a marginalized community, but it only takes a little effort to empathize and understand what someone else is going through. Being a good ally means moving through the world simply by treating the next person the way you want to be treated.

Your actions don't have to be these big, over-the-top, grand gestures. We've often found it funny that when people learn that we're gay, they think that they have to go out and buy rainbow pins and declare their love for us on a T-shirt. We ain't asking you to go out and become an overnight activist. In the same way that you would support a good friend, those are the same actions that you would take with someone in our community. It can be as simple as taking a few hours out of your day to show up for a local LGBTQIA+ event or donating to your local LGBTQIA+ center or queer-owned business. It all matters. If and when you feel called to do more, ask questions and see what people in the community you're seeking to support need the most. Don't be a bystander—be smart and think through what the best ways are for you to be a great ally for our community.

Making the changes that we believe are necessary within the next decade starts by showing up and being active at the polls. We really do have the power to change the world around us by the people we vote for, and when we see injustices happening in our communities, we do have a responsibility to call them out and make things right. You can do something today to make sure that every family and every person has the right to live and love out loud.

Acknowledgments

First and foremost, we need to acknowledge all the brave souls that came before us who stood in the face of discrimination and said "ENOUGH!" Without your sacrifices to advance the LGBTQIA+ community we would not be able to live out loud or have the family we'd always dreamt of. If there is any one piece of wisdom you take away from this book, we hope it is the realization that love is the purest thing you can experience in life, and it will always conquer hate. Through every adversity we have ever faced, it was love that brought us through.

Thank you to our amazingly fierce manager, Christina Jones, of Digital Brand Architects, for opening up this door from the very beginning. You have transformed our lives in ways we could never have imagined, and we can't even put into words our gratitude.

Thank you to our literary agent, Nena Madonia, for being the champion of our dreams and for guiding us through this process. Your genuineness, passion, and assurance are why this book is here today.

To our brilliant editor, Amina Iro, thank you. From the very beginning *Love Out Loud* resonated with you in ways only we know. You saw the vision and helped us tremendously to frame it in a way we could truly be proud of. We would also like to thank the Legacy Lit team at Hachette Book Group for helping to bring this vision to life. Your dedication to ensuring that the stories of underrepresented, marginalized, and diverse groups are told is unmatched. We cannot express our gratitude enough, not only for ourselves, but also for all the other authors whose stories you have helped to tell. You guys are Real Ones.

Another big thank-you, to Leah Lakins of Fresh Eyes Editorial, for helping us to get our most vulnerable thoughts onto the paper. The countless hours you spent writing and especially working around our crazy schedule is appreciated more than you know.

We would also like to thank the amazing Kristina Grish, for the hours of listening and believing in us! Your friendship both professionally and personally has been truly a godsend!